THE MODERN SCHISM

THE MODERN SCHISM

Three Paths to the Secular

MARTIN E. MARTY

1817

HARPER & ROW, PUBLISHERS
New York and Evanston

FIRST U.S. EDITION

LIBRARY OF CONGRESS CATALOG CARD NUMBER: 74-85042

CONTENTS

6   *Contents*

To Professors
Sidney E. Mead, Daniel J. Boorstin, James H. Nichols
at the University of Chicago
1954-56

I

The Modern Schism ·
An Episode in the West

At one point in history, God and the priests
seemed to become superfluous, yet the world went
on as before.   *Eric Hoffer*

A schism is a 'division into mutually opposing parties of a body of
persons that have previously acted in concert'. In the middle decades
of the nineteenth century people who had acted in concert to make
up Christendom finally divided into mutually opposing parties;
one set devoted itself to religious and ecclesiastical concerns. The
other was increasingly preoccupied with the secular.

The reality of the secular has recently come to obsess Western
religious thinkers. The term, unsatisfying though it may be, has
established itself, must be lived with and understood. It is destined
to have as many meanings and shadings as the word 'religious',
over against which it is usually posed. To avoid confusion, in this
book the secular will be spoken of in the senses defined by the
Oxford English Dictionary.

Secular means 'of or pertaining to the world'; 'belonging to the
world and its affairs as distinguished from the church and religion
. . . Chiefly used as a negative term, with the meaning non-
ecclesiastical, non-religious, or non-sacred'; 'of or belonging to the
present or visible world as distinguished from the eternal or spiritual
world; temporal, worldly'.

The novelty in modern theologians' use of the term has been in
their ability to take it from negative contexts and to give 'secular'
a positive force. In part this change may have revealed nothing
more than a coping with destiny, throwing in the towel, or making
a virtue of necessity. They seemed to be unable to fight off secularizing agents: why not join them? More realistically, they recognized
that what religion talked about also was 'of or pertaining to the

world' – that in the Jewish and Christian scheme of things, the world was the milieu of the ultimate drama of life.

However creative this about-face by religious thinkers has been, it has often been marked by an over-simple understanding of secularization as a determining process and a single all-encompassing style. Secularization, in the writings of many theological and social thinkers, has a single dimension and direction. On the basis of such a wholistic approach many go on to extrapolate from present tendencies to predict, project, or prophesy an over-simple fulfilled secular future.

This book differs from such accounts and attempts and is designed as a historian's contribution to the understanding of secular reality as it has unfolded in a pluralist world. It avoids all comment about the future. Instead, by studying a decisive moment in modern culture, it will attempt to establish that the secular has been approached and appropriated in vastly differing ways in different segments of the larger culture and that these ways have determined understanding during the subsequent century down to at least the recent past.

The very first attempts to express utter (maximal) secularity – which some call secularism – involved a formal and unrelenting attack on gods and churches and a studied striving to replace them. This derives chiefly from the mid-nineteenth century continental experience and was uncongenial to the experience of secular forces in Anglo-America even then, as it did not explain many current modes in England or the United States.

Another approach was expressive of mere secularity. In it, gods and churches were increasingly ignored and men made fewer systematic attempts to replace them. The mundane order, with its many details and attractions, drew their attention. While something of this style was evident all over the West, it characterized England in an age of industrial change and religious doubt.

Meanwhile, only a minority on the east side of the Atlantic, but a majority in the partly derivative American culture, adhered to inherited religions; this majority, however, transformed them so significantly (if subtly) that one may speak of the change as one of controlled (ambiguous) secularization.

To Speak of Schism

These three characteristic experiences make up part of what I am calling the Modern Schism,* an episode in the cultural and spiritual history of the West, and one which has had fateful consequences. The adjective Modern and the noun Schism both deserve examination.

During the middle decades of the nineteenth century (from approximately 1830 to 1870), the Western nations went 'over the hump of transition' towards a new ethos of industrial enterprise, urbanization and nationalism, accompanied by locally varying programmes or creeds like liberalism, evolutionism, socialism, or historicism. These and other 'isms' helped constitute the modern world and made up what Robert Binkley once called 'the pitiless and persistent' rivals of the twentieth-century Church.

Today, many reach for the prefix 'post-' to suggest that it is precisely that modern world which is breaking up. Post-modern, post-civilized, post-industrial, and post-historic have been offered in the era post-post-Christianity as signs that technology, the media, racism, affluence, and new revolutions are forcing still another perception of reality on men. That may be true. This historical analysis is designed to help people understand the modern world with which they have been living. If that world is indeed disintegrating, it is no less important to recognize what is going, for the raw material of the new will come from what has been inherited from the past.

The choice of the term Schism was designed to indicate that secularization did *not* mean the disappearance of religion so much as its relocation. It may be argued that the components of modernity (like industrialism) have served to diminish the institutions and qualify the claims of religions, but the latter have for the most part not disappeared, as other components (like nationalism) demonstrate their durability.

The Modern Schism affected most the inherited religion of the West, Christianity. Its upheaval may be compared to the effects of a geological 'fault' on glacial terrain. It can result in a violent shift, so that the old main body dwindles and continues its way while the newly created slope attracts a larger fresh mass. Back from metaphor: something of this kind of fault and shift is represented in the

* These words will be capitalized throughout.

dramatic battles of Europe. Or it can result in a milder shift, so that a great deal of mixed moraine is left on the landscape. The Jewish-Christian heritage makes up something like this mixture on the American landscape as a result of the nineteenth-century changes.

In Christian history a number of previous faults and shifts had occurred. In the first century, one may speak of a schism between the Jewish host culture and religion and the new Christian faith and culture. Ten centuries later came the split between Eastern and Western Christians. (This story deals exclusively with the West, but the slightly later history of Russia or the enduring struggles in the Near East would, upon examination, demonstrate that a schism has indeed affected the surviving Christian Church there, too.)

A third schism (the dictionary also speaks of schism as 'a breach of the unity of the visible Church . . .', specifically, 'a state of divided allegiance in Western Christendom') was Western, between Protestants and Catholics in the sixteenth century. What historians have called the Renaissance and the Enlightenment, however, were steps or stages in the final kind of schism, in which Christianity and the culture which it had largely informed went separate ways.

In such a reading, as the first historian to use the term, Jules Michelet (in 1855),[1] saw it, the Renaissance implied the discovery of the world, of man; it was the genesis of that modern 'post-Christian' cosmos with which subsequent Westerners have learned to live. Similarly, the Enlightenment – so named by its advocates – was a full programme of scepticism about historic Christian claims, attacks on Christian institutions and power, and attempts to replace the Christian interpretations of life.

The Modern Schism was a more complex, extensive, and devastating event for Christians. The earlier two episodes were followed by some sort of revival of Christian culture. The third has not been. To report this way is not to engage in prediction that there could not be but merely to repeat that there has not been, and that there have been few signs of culture-wide achievements so far as reinstatement of the Christian culture are concerned.

The attempt to tell the story of the Modern Schism necessarily blends 'hard news' history with interpretive or symbolic history. That is, the Renaissance or Enlightenment, the Age of Revolution or the Industrial Revolution, the epoch of Christendom or Western

Civilization did not 'occur' in the same way that the Battle of Hastings or the Defenestration at Prague occurred. They are the necessary and partly artificial constructs which historians need to tell their stories.

Because such symbolic history can lead it can also mislead, and historians are wary when they write it. But they all do, at least modestly, whenever they introduce, conclude, select, point, generalize, or interpret. Some do so overtly in their book and chapter titles; for others the construct is disguised, locked into the structure of sentences and nuances of phrase. The 'hard news' events – what men said and wrote and did day by day – must themselves be the judges of interpretive histories, lest 'symbolic' history screen out uncongenial aspects of reality and history become laws or doctrines.

To my knowledge, the story of the Modern Schism as an episode has not previously been told, though the literature on its components is enormous. Why has it been neglected? For one thing, as a result of the Schism: secular historians have often neglected the enduring role of religion in modern culture, and religious historians have often contented themselves with living in the private ecclesiastical world. (Even to speak of secular historians and religious historians demonstrates a dimension of the schism.)

The Modern Schism has been overlooked because it is often seen as a mere consequence or after-effect of the Enlightenment. This book will show, I hope, that anything but that is the case, though in boxing terms one might speak of Enlightenment and Modern Schism as a 'one-two punch' interrupted by a period of revival and religious reformulation.

Another consequence of modernity for historians has been their tendency to write on merely national lines (lines no less artificial for the task of understanding than are attempts to write on the bases of smaller regions or larger cultures!) and thus to overlook culture-wide coincidences and confluences. That countless historians have been discussing various aspects of this great cultural shift, however, is clear from the bibliographical essay at the end of this volume.

WHEN, WHERE, HOW?

The narrative and argument of this book can be tested in various ways. First, conventionally applicable to all historical writing: Does it tell its story well, on the basis of proper evidence? The other two major tests relate to the argument of the book. One must ask: did the Modern Schism constitute an episode, occurring *when* we say it did? That is, had the Enlightenment and Revolutionary shock to Christianity been blunted or by-passed by the intervening political restorations, reactions, and reconstructions and by the religious revivals, reawakenings, renewals, reformations, and re-formulations? (Did, in short, enough hard news occur in the 1820s through to the 1840s that we can legitimately speak of the begin-ning of a new movement in the West?)

Similarly, had enough occurred by around 1870 – so far as the new dogmas of nationalism, socialism, historism, liberalism, secu-larism, and industrialism were concerned – to warrant our speaking of a fulfilled episode which had set the terms for much of the subsequent relation of religion to the rest of the culture?

The other test is based on the question, did the Modern Schism occur *where* we say it did and in *ways* detailed in what follows? There is no attempt here to say that the great fault or shift did not occur anywhere but in the nations whose experiences are detailed. We have chosen these concentrations because Western Europe and Anglo-America were at that time pioneers in steps which made them the first 'developed' industrial nations, and be-cause so much of the subsequent plot of history follows their fate as they confronted what were the later and less developed ones.

As for the ways, there is no attempt to be exhaustive. There are as many ways as there are men and movements. On these pages we have taken what Jacob Burckhardt called *Querdurchschnitten*,[2] 'transverse sections of history in as many directions as possible'. ('Above all, we have nothing to do with the philosophy of history,' he went on – and I could, for this book at least.) Or, to vary the picture by reference to a metaphor used a century later by Lionel Thornton,[3] we shall perform 'the operation of taking soundings' as St Paul and his shipmates did (Acts 27.27, 28) to determine their location. All historians, by their choice of topics, take transverse sections of history, or soundings. The test here will be: how faithfully do ours reproduce the experiences of important repre-sentatives of European and Anglo-American cultures?

Thus, if Americans can be demonstrated to have welcomed, or

at least encountered, god-killing anti-Christian advocates on their own soil or if the continental secularists can be shown to have made the transition without such figures, there is reason to challenge part of the narrative.

This book condenses materials explored in a score of seminars and a small library of documents and books. I have tried to keep it brief so that it can be suggestive. Rudyard Kipling once said that he would hold his stories up to the wind and shake them so that the superfluous would fall out and then he would publish what was left over. Most of what fell out here did not feel superfluous for me and much of it will show up, no doubt, in proposed subsequent detailed studies of the era which I hope to develop in future years. This account of the Modern Schism is a first word, not a last word. The bibliographical essay is made up for the most part of monographs and other books which tend to reinforce, illumine, or enlarge upon points in this one. If *The Modern Schism* looks audacious in its attempt to style the period and discern some modes, it is modest in its basic intention: to plot the course for further study and to contribute to an understanding of the complex of paths to the secular taken by predecessors.

DECLINE AND FALL FOR WESTERN RELIGION?

Several words are in order for those who wonder about the religious implications of this narrative. Because it accents the triumph of the secular, it may look like a story of decline and fall, pure and simple, for religion. After all, in this episode the faith of nineteen centuries and the Christian culture of fifteen centuries met new and effective opposition.

Such a decline-and-fall judgment is valid if one sees the unfolding of the secular order as always and only a misfortune for faith. Such a view is not necessary. For example, one of the most decisive steps taken on the paths to the secular was *legal* secularization, including various kinds of separation of Church and state. Most Western Christians (and certainly most American believers) regard such separation as a boon to both faith and culture. They welcome, similarly, the moves from alchemy and astrology and medieval views of the body towards modern sciences and medicine as liberating. For whatever problem each of these raised for believers in their time, most Christian theologians today would endorse them and even try to relate them to the positive themes of Biblical and Christian witness.

This may be doom and gloom or decline and fall, secondly, if one is a 'triumphalist' Christian who sees his faith dependent on the 'tall towers of total Christendom', or if he is a determinist about the future based on one or another of the lines of secular trend today. This book is open about the future; with Nietzsche it regards man at least in part as 'an indeterminate being', who will unfold in the light of changing values in changing environments. It is in this sense that with Burckhardt we have nothing to do with the kind of philosophy of history that deals with the future as if it had already occurred, or with past and present as if we knew the final outcome of history, or history as a whole. Here we part company with those theologians who write as if they 'know' that secular man (in the form they describe), is the essential and finally fulfilled man or that secular culture as now depicted is the fruition of all culture. ('Just as if the world and its history had existed merely for our sakes! For everyone regards all times as fulfilled in his own, and cannot see his own as one of many passing waves', scolded Burckhardt.)[4]

This book could belong to the 'decline and fall' school if it manifested a masochistic spirit or a sense of *Schadenfreude*, a rejoicing in the misfortunes of blundering nineteenth-century churchmen. Rather, it attempts to deal with them without condescension and in the context of possibilities that looked open to them, while giving due attention to their survival and achievements. If a man wishes to be the judge of the past, he can hand out plenty of good and bad grades to people in a time called 'the great century' by Christians because of their successes and by non-Christians because of theirs, a time also mourned over for its egregious failings by Christian and non-Christian alike.

In his eleventh thesis on Feuerbach, Karl Marx exclaimed: 'the philosophers have only *interpreted* the world in various ways: the point, however, is to *change* it.'[5] In an attempt to concentrate on people to whom initiative in history was passing we shall look not only at intellectuals but also at industrial workers – and not only at both of them but also at the complex and varied middle classes where the churches had more successes. We are suggesting by this that effective religion or its surrogates or successors somehow provide adherents with interpretations of their cosmos as well as with power for changing the world. How men set out to interpret and change the world in the nineteenth century has determined much of the fate of the world in the twentieth.

II

Towards Utter Secularity ·
A Clash of Doctrines on the Continent

> . . . the Church had fallen from first to last place
> in European leadership. The secular dogmas that
> triumphed against it in those decades were destined
> to stand for the remainder of the nineteenth century
> and into the twentieth as its most pitiless and
> persistent rivals.
>   . . . the breach of the Catholic Church with the do-
> minant secular forces approached the dimensions of
> a schism in civilization . . .   *Robert C. Binkley*

Whenever men have wished to see the Western world turn utterly
secular, they have devoted themselves to devastating and then re-
placing Christendom. By Christendom we mean that system of
Christian teachings fused with institutions which penetrated most
sectors of Western life after the fourth century A.D., a system which
provided the population with a scheme for organizing and interpreting their social and personal life.

Utter secularity would mean maximal secularity. That is, its pro-
ponents cannot let Christendom die a natural death; they cannot be
content to watch its doctrines lose their power or stand by to
see its forms lose their attraction. Instead, they must see the Christian syntheses and structures as being the enemy of values and must
work to destroy them. Destruction may imply frontal assault on a
living entity or mopping up operations when its death impends.
It may force people to use appropriate counterpower when
Christendom was authentically potent or may allow them to make
a bogey out of vestigial Christianity in order to advance their own
causes.

In the French Enlightenment of the eighteenth century the
frontal attack included the cry, 'Crush the infamous thing!', along
with numerous alternative proposals for syntheses and schemes for
life organized apart from Christian symbols. A clerical society

bred anti-clericalism: a Christian dogmatic skein evoked an anti-Christian one. After the Enlightenment in France and across much of Western Europe there followed a brief period of reaction and rebuilding on the part of romantic Christians.

Then, in the middle decades of the nineteenth century the frontal attack included the proclamation, 'God is dead!' It was uttered by a great variety of people for numbers of often conflicting purposes. Whatever else they meant by the phrase and its numerous paraphrases, they made clear that they regarded the Christian legacy as representing bad faith, not faith; enslavement, not freedom; falsehood, not truth.

After the mid-nineteenth century conflict and cultural shift there have been minor, isolable, and sporadic Christian revivals in Western Europe. But there has not been a general recovery, a marked desire on the part of the majority of the people to return to the Christian faith or on the part of the whole culture to return to Christian norms. The mid-nineteenth century, then, represents the Modern Schism. In those years the modern world – the world of nationalism, socialism, communism, industrialism – was put together autonomously even as it permitted the heirs of Christendom to survive in carefully sequestered corners of their old empire to deal with rigidly segregated aspects of life.

This characteristic continental version of the Modern Schism differs considerably from contemporaneous realities in England and the United States, two other areas of industrial and political development. England knew a few minor god-killers and now and then provided a home for continental ideas or advocates of ideas about the deaths of God, Church, and Christian culture. But twentieth-century heirs of the legacy of those years do not have to deal seriously with the thought about the death of God in England. Rather, they have to reckon with people who began to ignore Christian claims, to become impervious to them; people who found that God, Church, and Christian teaching were superfluous in their thought and action. To people excited by a clash of doctrines, the British experience of drift and doubt seems drab and bland – a minimal approach which might be called 'mere secularity'.

The continent, of course, also saw such drift and doubt. Not all thinkers in France or Germany were as sure of themselves as

Auguste Comte and Karl Marx, Ernest Renan and Ludwig Feuerbach, to name just a few of the new doctrinaires. Some of them merely let faith fade away and die and, like Englishmen, let the ancient religious concerns wither during their preoccupations with other matters. Not all common people of Europe raged against God, Church, and doctrine. Many of them found that these simply no longer helped them construe reality in the way they had served their fathers. The industrial age numbered millions who found the church unable to adapt, who found it pointless. They will not be forgotten in this study, but their contribution to later problems and possibilities is secondary to that of their contemporaries who waged war on Christendom and tried to replace it.

In the United States, god-killers and atheists were rare; infidelity was not socially acceptable in a society which was moving towards an ever higher degree of participation in the life of religious institutions. 'Utter secularity' – the maximal programme which involved witness to the death of God – is virtually unheard of in the nineteenth-century United States. During the mid-century decades, however, as the United States industrialized and turned urban, it underwent drastic religious change. An autonomous culture was developing. Yet it was screened from view in part because of religious leaders' ability to disguise the secularizing change by adapting and reapplying symbols of Christian reminiscence and continuity at significant points of change.

On the continent, Christian churches also survived, though they dwindled in proportion to the population during the century of rapid growth in America. Millions remained faithful. They, like people in the new world, found religious spokesmen who assured them that the religious changes and accommodations they were making were legitimate by Christian standards – that they were what God had had in mind all along. (This was particularly true when clerics applied Christian norms and symbols to justify the new secular nationalisms which were actually becoming rival religions in Europe.)

Without forgetting the residual powers of continental Christianity to hold the attention of some of the faithful and to convince them that their secularizing moves could be controlled by the manipulation of Christian symbols, students of Western European history do not find this situation to be characteristic, nor do heirs of nineteenth-century Europe devote themselves to facing the problem of disguised and masked secularity, as they find it valid to concentrate on the more devastating doctrinal clashes which centred in the prophecy concerning the death of God.

But God, Church, and traces of Christian culture did not disappear; disappearance is not the point of the observation about a move towards utter secularity. If it were, it would be pointless to speak of the Modern Schism. For a schism implies a splitting between two parties, a division into two entities. On one side, Christian churches, teachings, and faith remained. On the other, there appeared an alternate set of reasonably thought out and vigorously contended arguments for metaphysical or social doctrines, creeds, and systems.

THE OLDEST DAUGHTER: FRANCE

Any exploration of dreams that a united Christendom or Christian synthesis might survive has to begin with Roman Catholicism. In the nineteenth century, as later, it still represented majority Christianity, a world-wide (catholic) institution, and the centre of international European Christian consciousness.

The drama of Catholicism's encounter with secularizing forces in the nineteenth century is viewed in France as well as anywhere. Catholicism was a small minority presence in the Anglo-American and Scandinavian worlds. But in France, the 'oldest daughter of the Church', it had remained in the majority after the Reformation and had lived a creative life semi-independent of Roman claims.

The instance of setbacks in Italy, heartland of the papacy, would be almost equally revealing. There, as in France, new social doctrines were fashioned to beguile the faithful or to provide surrogate religions for the faithless. There, as almost everywhere in mid-century European Catholic countries, the militant and largely successful nationalists were anti-clerical and often anti-religious.

'Young Italy', 'the Risorgimento' and other movements working for the unification of Italy and the rise of modern nationalism became problems to the clergy and the Church. The leaders like Giuseppe Mazzini, Giuseppe Garibaldi, and Camillo Cavour on one hand, or almost any memorable revolutionary on the other, turned out to be rebellious sons of the Church. The united Italy of 1861 or 1870 provided anything but a hospitable centre for the beleaguered but belligerent papacy at the time characterized by the anti-modern Syllabus of Errors (1864) or the first Vatican Council in 1870.

Two or three centuries earlier the story would have had to concentrate on the Iberian peninsula. But for Spain and Portugal, as for Italy, the imperial hour had largely passed; no longer do they deserve international focus of attention, nor is their legacy for the twentieth century so traceable. Not that the story differs markedly there: the Church was more militant and repressive than it was or could afford to be in France. There the new social and national movements were ordinarily anti-clerical and were offered as alternatives to Christendom's claims. But these, frankly, play minor roles in the story of religion in developing nations in the nineteenth century.

In the East, the Western Catholic Church had met rebuff. In the nineteenth century a few unsuccessful tentative Roman Catholic moves towards the Orthodox homelands were made, but there were no memorable institutional breakthroughs or major ecumenical ventures across the lines of the millennium-old East-West schism. Roman Catholicism had had to settle for being provincially Western and then to find new territories in colonial outposts of the West. There the Catholic drama *vis-à-vis* secularizing trends would be worked out.

In its main centres, the Catholic Church knew almost nothing but hardship, setback, rejection, or neglect during that century. Ironically, it was most often most nearly free to live its own life in non-Catholic nations like England after Emancipation in 1829 and in the United States, despite Nativists' hostility to new immigrant masses at mid-century. Most people who stand in Protestant or secular liberal academic traditions as they survey the nineteenth century political experience of Catholicism have much unlearning to do first. The Church of that century, so often portrayed to them as an all-powerful monolith intent only on determining which political choice out of many it should take, was actually bargaining from weakness. The papacy seems often to have been hanging by a thread, as it were. Many of the most strident claims of Pius IX, the pope who dominated the era, have to be understood not as the assertions of existing power but rather as defensive, sometimes bluffing and sometimes panicky reaches for power and prestige.

Ireland? Should it be the centre of the Catholic story? There, because of the Catholic Church's identification with new nationalist aspirations, the Church lived an aggressive life, hampered less by alternative systems than by the realities of poverty and famine – and the proximity and power of England. The modern Irish Church itself lacked the theological and institutional heritage which would have permitted it an easy transition to modernity. In Scotland, the natives' concept of a national – and non-Roman – *Ecclesia Scoticana* kept Catholicism in the minority. The story in Belgium, defined as an overwhelmingly Catholic country in the partition of 1830, provides interesting footnotes to the French story but holds less independent interest.

In France, then, and to a lesser degree in Germany, one expects to find the dramatic story and is not disappointed after a reading of the record. There the legacy of the anti-Catholic Enlightenment lived on; there the agonies of the Church in the French Revolution remained vivid. And in France, too, there was enough Catholic revival in the early decades of restoration or reaction and throughout the century to warrant observing the Church as one of the two parties to the schism.

The Gallican Church makes possible many observations of Roman adaptation to modernity in affairs of state. The Revolution had already effected legal secularization in decisive areas: no longer were the rites of passage in French life all under the control of the clergy. The religious orders had been banished or hampered. The numbers of clergy had been cut, and many Revolutionary resolutions left legal restrictions on churches which were not lifted by Napoleon and his successors, who enjoyed leaving the Church in a subservient role. Full 'separation of Church and state' was not to come in France throughout the century and at mid-century, particularly in the field of education, middle-class reactionary Catholics were able actually to make gains in their legal status.

Despite that one counter-sign, it was clear that the papacy would not be free to dominate or call the signals in France. It was reduced to bargaining through concordats with the autonomous national powers and had to comment on the movement of politics through a series of encyclicals which might still stir the faithful. But they did not awe and terrify statesmen in the way that interdicts and excommunications could in earlier centuries.

In France, after the Enlightenment and the Revolution, one can keep an eye on every kind of continuing revolution and restoration and observe a novel impact on the Church. There industrialism occurred (though not quite on the pace of that in England, America, or Germany); the cities grew; integral and doctrinaire nationalism developed; socialism met with some favour; alternative secular religions were periodically advocated. There, too, enough of the faithful remained faithful to help heighten the tension between the old and the new. During and just after the Restoration (1814-1830) the papacy cheered France's new national spirit, but by 1870 Rome had reason to fear it. During these years, despite all the shouting, the papal position over against France was weakened and had become defensive.

THE POLITICAL CHURCH

Nineteenth-century Catholicism in France began in a relationship of pathos. On July 15, 1801, the pope signed a concordat which was to establish the fundamental relation of crown to papacy for over a century. On paper the concordat looked creative; actually it left the papacy at the mercy of the French ruler, who would honour or dishonour the agreement from time to time, according to whim and to serve the purposes of his own advantage.

Napoleon had shown how he could exploit religion. 'How are we to create social customs?' He provided the answer to his own question, 'There is only one way and that is to re-establish religion. . . . How are we to create order in a State without a religion?' Then in words that would have provided fuel for Marxist-style criticism: 'No society can exist without inequality of wealth, and inequality of wealth is not possible without religion.'

Napoleon, who had said he could be an atheist in Paris and a Muslim in Cairo, knew that people needed religion and 'religion must be controlled by the government'. He knew that he needed the pope to bring order and therefore worked for the Concordat of 1801. Pius VII was pleased with the arrangement, for it promised rebuilding after much of the Revolution's damage to the Church.

Meanwhile in France, Napoleon was being built up by fawning supporters so that he took on a quasi-religious status in opposition to orthodox Catholicism. The bishops allowed him a place in the Catechism and even in the church year by contriving a false etymology for a saint's name to give Napoleon nominal holy antecedency. So Catholicism entered the century in a position dependent upon the secular power, and the secular authority was endowed with a theological sanction. As for the clergy? 'These religious will be most useful to me in Asia, Africa, and America.'[1]

The restoration of the Ancien Régime between 1814 and 1830 allowed for a different liaison between throne and altar and a somewhat less degraded situation for the clergy. But many hierarchical spokesmen permitted no Christian judgment on the throne. Thus the Bishop of St-Brieuc asked the faithful to be obedient to the civil ruler because he 'derives his sovereign power from above, however evil his morals . . . whatever the abuses, apparent or real, of his government'.[2]

The climate of reaction to the Revolution did favour efforts towards renewal of the idea of Christendom and a number of conservatives dreamed of restoring the old order around a revitalized Church. Joseph de Maistre, Vicomte de Bonald, François de Chateaubriand and others had visions of a traditionalist constitutional realm which could begin to restore Catholic Europe to what they pictured it had once been. The romantic Chateaubriand may be compared to Sir Walter Scott for, like Scott, he evoked the aesthetic delights and the way of life of the Middle Ages and used these to inspire others to measure the decay of the modern period.

The clerical policy of Villèle, minister under Louis XVIII and Charles X in the 1820s, stimulated anti-clerical reaction. This anti-clericalism came to characterize not only French revolutionary sentiment but also much middle-class republican idealism. Villèle had permitted the clericals to regain their hold in education and they pursued their anti-secular policies with an alienating kind of fanaticism. With friends like these, the Church hardly needed enemies.

The experiences under Napoleon, in the Restoration, and in the hands of the romantic conservatives, did not prepare the Church to be ready for the new Europe in which factory workers were eventually to beckon for attention and in which liberal ideologues and non-Christian socialists or utopians would offer opposing schemes.

Now and then someone would come on the scene to set forth programmes for adaptation and change, someone who could foresee modern problems. But none of these was able to reshape French Catholicism. Best remembered of these is the tragic Hugues-Félicité Robert de Lamennais (1782-1854), who had been first a priest but who became a gifted maverick political agitator and journalist.

Lamennais in effect contended for a twofold programme: he must see the Church in France lifted from its supine and servile status. The way to do that was to exalt the papacy, to be ultra-montane in policy. The other part of the plan called for recognition of the needs of workers and others whose social status was complicated by industrial change. He was not well-informed about their conditions, but he did recognize that they were being exploited. Like most social Catholics – or social Christians in general – in the nineteenth century, Lamennais did not come forward with a complete plan for societal overhaul. Rather, he looked for a great extension of charities. He had a profound faith in the common people, a faith based more on a naturally sympathetic heart than on real contact with them. His were intellectual and abstract loyalties. To non-Catholic latter-day liberals his looks like an improbable mix: to advocate what looked like religious institutional conservatism in order to effect a kind of politically liberal social policy.

Such a programme made sense in Lamennais' day; he had consistently fought what he thought was the atheism of the state. His lever for religious liberty was to be papal authority. Rome showed some early interest in Lamennais' theories, for they would have elevated the papacy to a new height. In *Des progrès de la Revolution* in 1829 he prophesied the forthcoming popular revolutions even as he set forth means for separating Church from state. With forward-looking but more moderate associates like Charles Montalembert and Jean Baptiste Lacordaire he seemed for a time to be making headway, but he became an embarrassment both to the papacy he was supporting and to the French state which was threatened by his calls for reform.

Lamennais convinced himself that the Pope would support his calls for freedom, and he went to Rome in 1832 to argue his case before Gregory XVI. But he was condemned, in general terms in 1832 and specifically in 1834. He left the Church, refusing its ministries, and choosing instead a kind of private Catholic pantheism.

Lamennais' career can be examined for the difficulties of the Church which it illumines. 'We are afraid of Liberalism; Catholicize it and society will be born again,' he had promised. After him, the Religion of Liberty, as it has been called, fell more and more into the hands of the non-religious and of anti-clericals. The papacy was not in a strong enough position to endorse even those who would elevate it at the expense of the alliance of throne and altar; French Catholicism was not ready to move with its prophets.

The parallel growth of modern religious nationalism and religious political conservatism became evident early. The papacy revealed how fearful of liberalism it was. When, after the Revolution of 1830, Belgium became independent and showed itself to be a Catholic nation, Rome, fearing that freemasonry must have been the only instigator of anything bearing the stamp of revolution, and resenting the constitution's separation of Church and State, was slow to recognize the nation and did not even send a nuncio to this Catholic country for a decade.

The Catholic experience with revolutions in these decades is consistently illuminating. The Church was always in a hurry to recognize legitimacies and to deal positively with conservative established authorities, however repressive they may be. The list of concordats designed to maintain the status quo in the 1850s is an impressive sign of this scurrying: with Spain in 1851 and 1859; with Austria, in 1855; with Württemberg in 1857 and Baden in 1859; finally, in the early 1860s, it made such agreements with half a dozen Latin-American nations. But Rome could somehow never anticipate or greet Revolution or even indicate its support of aspirant liberals.

Europeans tried to keep on speaking the new language, 'the language of happiness', and the call for freedom in numerous nineteenth-century revolutions. These occurred in France in 1830, over much of Europe in 1848, and again in France from 1848-51;

Hungary, Italy, Germany were involved with them in the late 1840s. In 1870 France was again stirred. Rome did not always actively oppose these revolutions, but it was eager to establish connections wherever and whenever reactionary forces gained control.

Wonder of wonders, the new Pope Pius IX was at first a liberal — or, at least, so it had been whispered. But liberalism died in this man who held longest tenure in the papal office, for he suffered personal inconvenience and agony in the revolution of 1848. In Italy, Spain, and the Piedmont, the progressing Carbonari were negative against the Church. None of the revolutions were, as such, anti-clerical or anti-religious, and lower-level priests sometimes aided rebels under the banner of 'Christ the Revolutionary'. But the tension between the papacy and revolutionary forces increased and the popes kept on stimulating 'the parties of order' over against most political, social, and industrial change. In Italy and France the state was secularized, or at least de-christianized. In Italy, after the Law of Guarantees, the pope was a self-named prisoner of the Vatican in 1871. In France the Law of Separation did not come until 1905, but the secularizing tendency was much older than that.

The diplomatic policies of the Vatican, in short, did not slow down political secularization. The German *Kulturkampf*, which Catholicism did manage to outlast in the 1870s, was a sign that support of conservative policies did not pay off for Rome in Germany. In 1867 the Austrian Concordat was denounced. The States of the Church were lost in the formation of modern Italy, and the Kingdom of Italy seized Rome. The Falloux Laws, part of a pro-Catholic middle class reaction to the Revolution of 1848, were countered by the Ferry Laws in the 1870s.

Men were speaking as Louis-Antoine de Saint-Just had prophesied they would, in the language of a new secular call for freedom, divorced from historic Christian theological roots. But this language often took on a sort of alternative religious cast itself. Many sought a bourgeois non-Christian morality which Christian conservatives found superficially congenial. But new words also symbolized new realities for which the Church was not ready: sociology, ideology, the individual, the middle class, technology: these were among the new coinages.

De Tocqueville summarized the situation as he accounted for what looked like a return to faith, but what he knew to be superficial. It had two causes, 'the fear of socialism which produces momentarily upon the middle classes an effect analogous to that which the French Revolution produced upon the upper classes': and 'the government of the *masses,* which for the present at least gives back to the Church and the landowners an influence which they have not had for sixty years'.[3]

Unfortunately for the future of Catholicism, the return to religion in such circumstances and the papacy's consistent support of conservative regimes took on frightening tones in the anti-liberal and anti-modern Syllabus of Errors of 1864. This document collected past writings condemning religious freedom, political republicanism and liberalism, and almost anything which could bear the name modern; warmed over and promulgated to the world, it alienated progressives in Europe and America. And in 1870 the proclamation of papal infallibility further divorced the papacy from forces which offered broader freedoms.

Meanwhile, France needed reform. In the Paris of 1836 it was estimated that 30,500 men had no regular work and another 50,000 were totally unemployed. And employed workers in the earlier days of industrialization had only meagre incomes. The slums in which they had to live offered no chance for healthy family life. Violence, disease, and exploitation were on all sides. A few Catholics stood in the tradition of Lamennais and tried to bring the attention of the Church to these problems.

For a brief moment in the 1840s, particularly through the offices of the journal *L'Ere Nouvelle,* numbers of French Catholics lined up with the French left wing. But reaction to the death of the courageous Archbishop of Paris in the Revolution of 1848 made it difficult for Catholics to be identified with socialists, and the group largely failed. In the 1850s, Catholicism was once again on the side of the newly secure middle classes and often thwarted the aspirations of workers and the poor.

Catholic theology and the Catholic faithful in general tended to accept the inevitability of widespread poverty and saw no reason to revise the historic teachings on the subject. Energies went chiefly, as they had in Protestant evangelicalism, into efforts which would alleviate individual poverty and improve the condition of victims of industrial change where personal vices were the problem and personal attention was the cure.

COMPETING SECULAR RELIGIONS

Post-Revolutionary France did not differ from Revolutionary France in one important respect: its citizens were not able to be de-christianized without having the crutch of some alternative faith. French intellectuals who wanted to extricate themselves from the embrace of the Church and to shrug off the dreams of the old Christendom often gravitated, as had the philosophers before them, to new schemes for organizing society and synthesizing all of life into neat systems. These systems were paratheological in nature. They have often been called secular religions. Many of these cosmic schemes provided an answer for everything and a ceremony for every occasion. In each, Christianity was either to be displaced or transformed beyond recognition.

Some of these new secular systems were born of the loss of Christian belief, as was the case with one devised by Edmond Scherer, a Calvinist turned doubter, or the more famed one of Ernest Renan, who renounced Catholicism in 1845 and tried to form a new community. Renan was less sanguine than most of the dreamers: 'I fail to see how, without the ancient dreams, the foundations of a happy and noble life are to be relaid.'[4] He hoped science would offer enlightenment. With Edgar Quinet, these men believed that something like historic religions was needed to direct all of life. Some called for faith in the new scientific manner, and called this faith Positivism.

The most celebrated of these cosmic prophets was Auguste Comte (1798-1857) who devised a 'positive philosophy'. His analysis of stages in history has influenced numerous later philosophers of history. He saw man and society moving inevitably from a theological stage past a metaphysical one to the final positive-scientific social physics which he favoured.

This band of prophets offered a cafeteria of delights. Claude Henri de Saint-Simon devised a whole sect, complete with hierarchies, in a reasonably pure attempt at aping the Church. 'The present generation,' he wrote, 'has caused to vanish from our books and our society that tone of frivolity and of pleasantry in matters of religious belief which the past generation flaunted.' He went on: 'It has been replaced by a general feeling of respect for religious ideas which is based on a conviction of their present need.'[5]

Barthelemy Enfantin, influenced by Near East deities, fashioned a syncretistic religion with sensual overtones. Etienne Cabet, trying to fuse Christianity with the secular faith of Communism, declared that Jesus Christ was a communist. Charles Fourier was chiefly a social utopian, proposing communities in France as well as in America. Pierre Leroux called his new scheme, in 1838, a 'religion of humanity'.

But the responding French public revealed in all this that, however scientific the intentions of these positivisms might have been, they were not able to shrug off metaphysics. Conventionally, in the place once occupied by God, they offered Integrating Absolutes or Supreme Beings. The eclectic Victor Cousin wanted all to recognize Love as a metaphysical deity. Jules Simon set out to humanize God. Ernest Renan saw God as the name for moral purpose. Progress was everywhere a part of the new theological systems.

In retrospect it is easy to smile at those who felt that positivism meant utter secularity and in the process fell victim to France's darling vice of system-building. It is similarly easy to see that Catholicism survived these eccentric new religions. From all of them, only a few ideas from Comte are to be reckoned with by serious people today. Yet these sometimes weird contrivances, by their very presence, suggested something of the dimensions of change in Europe. For many hopeful people, the conservative Church, jealous of her own prerogatives and failing to anticipate change or to identify with all but one of the new classes, no longer served for the organization of life, the interpretation of society, or change in the world.

Do these secular religions really demonstrate secularization? Perhaps everything that occurred through them might better be spoken of as religious change, for few of the prophets or followers became complete sceptics or atheists. What they were engaged in was the offering of new alternatives to exhausted Christendom. options which contrasted with what they regarded to be a spent theological lore and political heritage. It is safe to speak of them as revealing not the hesitant disbelief in Christianity seen in the sixteenth or seventeenth century or the infamy-crushing rage of the Enlightenment era, so much as the self-assured conviction that Christianity had become self-evidently irrelevant to human purpose and progress. Regrettably, these were often answered only with strident apologetics by journalists like Louis Veuillot. It was not a great age for Christian apology or reasoned reply.

INSIDE CATHOLICISM

This is not to say that residual Catholicism did not produce a rather varied private ecclesiastical life in these years. Not all of the Church's efforts were devoted to working out liaisons with thrones, denouncing modernity, resisting revolutions, supporting reactionary causes, or fighting off secular prophets. The parish system, in spite of the strains of urbanization, survived and many kept going to church. These were not years of creative theological endeavour but there were significant practical experiments with the life of the Church. While Veuillot shouted that the sceptics had succeeded, 'The people – not the whole of the people, through the grace of God, but an appreciable section of them, the work-men, the townsfolk, those who read and discuss politics – this part of the people lost their faith',[6] it was true that a majority stayed with the Church.

The religious orders, suppressed in the Revolution, and the ranks of the clergy, depleted at that time, saw gains in the nine-teenth century. The number of members in religious congregations, male and female, grew from 37,300 in 1851 to 106,900 in 1861 and to 157,900 in 1877! The annual number of vocations for secular clergy grew from 1,309 in 1847 to 1,753 in 1869, though it had dropped back to 1,582 in 1878. Liturgical reform occurred under men like Father Prosper Louis Pasqual Guéranger at Solesmes. Trappists and Carthusians experienced revival. Jean-Baptiste Lacordaire led a renewal in preaching. The Salesians of Don Bosco, under John Bosco, formed an agency that can be compared to the Protestant Salvation Army, to deal with the needs of the urban poor in direct ways. The 'White Fathers' of Charles Lavigerie matched Protestant energies in their African missions.

This was the century of the Sacred Heart in popular piety. The vision of a simple girl at Lourdes in 1858 gave impetus to Marian devotion. Jean Baptiste Marie Vianney, the Curé of Ars, a small village, served as a saintly model for quiet pastors. What the Church lacked was a cast of apologists, theologians, social thinkers, people who could relate the old faith to the modern world. Without them, the internal revivals of the Church were limited in scope and duration. Yet these revivals are part of the story and they reveal how it could be that the Church survived at all, to serve as one party to the Modern Schism.

French Protestantism, a rather small minority, was in no position to counteract the public secularizing trends. Now and then, as in the case of the noted statesman, François Guizot, a Protestant could rise to high position, but such rare instances did not provide Protestants with the security to encourage many independent thinkers and Guizot, who was congenial to Catholics, was a typical conservative. He did recognize that the intellectual hegemony of Catholicism had come to an end, but he was uneasy about the new 'moral' (read: social) sciences and literature that took its place. 'The excessive confidence in human intelligence, human pride, pride of spirit – let me call these things by their names – are the malady of our times, the cause of a great part of our errors and our evils.'[7]

The Protestants of the *Reveil*, the French Awakening which extended also to Switzerland, like their Anglo-American counterparts, worked some wonders inside the churches. They contented themselves with benevolent and humanitarian activities inside the given and accepted social realm rather than undertaking fundamental criticism of society. The admirable Alexander Vinet, who spoke of socialist sources in Christianity, was wary of contemporary socialism and, referring to the masses who were turning democratic, was reported to have declared in 1837, 'barbarians are coming not from the North but from below our feet'.[8]

BALANCE SHEET ON FRANCE

A balance sheet on France during the decades from the Revolution of 1830 to the Commune and war of 1870-71 sees the Church in an ever more negative reaction to Europe's emerging forces. The Syllabus of Errors was characteristic of the official position. From the condemnation of Lamennais in the 1830s through the isolation of the Catholic socialists in the 1850s the Church demonstrated its fear of innovators.

The rise of modern political nationalism and the display of alternative secular religions alike revealed the limits placed by nineteenth-century men on Christian claims. The Christian fate in the world lay at best in the hands of meliorists, who accepted the new social contract as inevitable and then worked to make conditions in the debris of the industrial revolution more nearly bearable. Those who looked to the Church for interpretation of life in a time of change had to content themselves with inherited patterns devised for earlier social order. Those who looked to the Church as an agent of change in the world, as an inspirer of passion, were destined to be disappointed. The new urban types, the new workers, were misunderstood and their hopes were denied. French writers and intellectuals were increasingly secularized (although there was to be a minor revival through conversions to Catholicism early in the twentieth century). The Church survived but, in spite of the early nineteenth century reaction and restoration, it was not able to regain its place and the effects of the Revolution and the Modern Schism remain with the 'eldest daughter' of the Roman Catholic Church.

GERMAN CATHOLICISM

German Catholicism offers just enough distinctiveness to merit brief observation. Germany, of course, was not a modern national state through most of the century. Rather it was a loosely affiliated group of scores of territories, coming to national consciousness especially through the rise to power of Brandenburg-Prussia. These territories had not known a political upheaval comparable to the French Revolution, and German intellectuals liked to say that their *Aufklärung*, or Enlightenment, had served as a surrogate for or equivalent to Revolution. There had been a religious renewal and rebuilding early in the century, and Catholicism experienced a minor revival.

Church lands were secularized in 1803 through the *Reichs-deputationshauptschluss*, and in 1806 the age-old Holy Roman Empire came to a formal end. One would think that these events should have been traumatic to Catholics, for they symbolized further disintegration of the legal claims on German soil. Yet there was no great turmoil, perhaps because German Catholics lived in isolated islands of population within a Protestant majority and were in no position to make arrogant claims or to mourn the lost status since they had little to lose three centuries after the German Reformation.

A German Catholic revival which antedates the period under study occurred during the period of *Sturm und Drang* among German poets, dramatists, and intellectuals. Much of this happened under the aegis of Johann Michael Sailer (1751-1832), who attracted a number of gifted Catholics, many of them converts, to his circle. Friedrich Schlegel and the poet Novalis were among the well-known converts. In Johann Adam Möhler (1796-1838), German theology seemed to be coming into its own. Möhler at Tübingen anticipated some of the trends towards a developmental view of dogma and church life which were later extended independently in John Henry Newman's work and eventually sidetracked in the Modernist movement.

Möhler, aware of and influenced somewhat by Hegel's philosophy of spirit, attempted to discern the unifying spirit of the age and saw the Church in organic terms. For him, tradition was 'the spiritual life-force which reproduces itself in the Church',[9] a view which led him to underplay the role of the Vatican as a power-centre in church history. Critical of Hegel, of the Protestant Friedrich Schleiermacher and of his own Protestant competitor, Ferdinand Christian Baur, the historian of dogma, Möhler at least knew how to locate the crucial intellectual problem for Catholics of his day in a time of historical relativism. He called for a return to the intentions of the church fathers as one means of restoring the identity and integrity of the Church in an erosive time. He feared that the newly assertive Church might seek the political route that it had in France, and was critical of political Catholicism; Möhler desired a co-ordinated, not a separated Church and state.

By the time of his premature death, his approach was already becoming dated as the German academies began to turn from the romantic Hegelian approach to development and to take up the scientific positivism of the neo-Kantian tradition. Not until the career of Ignaz von Döllinger did German Catholicism produce another first-rate intellectual. Von Döllinger was, like Möhler, a church historian. He began as a conservative ultramontane but was never attracted to romanticism, preferring a scientific approach to history. Lord Action was later to say that Döllinger 'thought it was Catholic to take ideas from history, and heresy to take them into it'.[10] But his critical spirit led him into difficulties. The move from Möhler to Döllinger reveals the pathos of German Catholicism as it faced change. Döllinger's attempt at objective inquiry led him to call into question many papal claims. The Syllabus of Errors condemned his approach and when he refused to assent to the doctrine of papal infallibility in 1870-71 he was excommunicated. 'The scales fell from my eyes.' He refused to join the dissident Old Catholic Church with which he was in general sympathy.

In its inability to follow Möhler, German Catholicism revealed its difficulty with the developmental approach. In its condemnation of Döllinger it repudiated the 'scientific', thus boxing itself in between the two main approaches to theological inquiry and innovation in a time of sudden cultural and intellectual change.

Hampered as it was in the intellectual realm, German Catholicism chose to be no more free or assertive in the political realm than French Protestantism, also a minority, had been. The great exception here, and the nearest German Catholicism came to producing a major figure who went against the trend of his Church in the social realm, was Wilhelm Emmanuel Ketteler, Bishop of Mainz after 1850. He anticipated social change, devoted his career to the attempt to free Catholicism from state domination, and worked as a moderate reformer in the public sphere.

Ketteler wrote *Die Arbeiterfrage und das Christenthum* in 1864, when the pope was busy drafting the Syllabus of Errors. This book indicated the degree of Ketteler's involvement with the new labouring masses and his calls for support of their legitimate causes. He was far from being a socialist in bishop's robes, but his identification with some workers and other victims of industrial change made him stand out. He was among those who opposed the decree on papal infallibility as being inopportune and only tardily and reluctantly assented to it when he had no choice. Nor did Ketteler lay down his weapons in the period of the *Kulturkampf* after 1870, when he again advocated the Catholic cause.

Neither the isolated intellectuals' attempts nor the championing of social causes by rarities like Ketteler were enough to bring about a real revival of German Catholicism, nor an extrication of that Church from dominance by the state in various German territories.

When one looks for vital, cultural life in mid-century Germany, it would never occur to one to look at the Catholic Church. This was unable, during the rise to modern nationhood in Germany, to serve as an interpreter of culture or an agent of change for the German majority. Instead it assumed an essentially passive role except when its own prerogatives were challenged, as in the *Kulturkampf*.

PROTESTANT GERMANY

That Germany should have played so fateful a part in the formation of modern ideology and religion does not seem surprising to people of the twentieth century, conscious as they are of Germany's national identity and cultural legacy. Yet for an eighteenth century person to look ahead, the possibility of a German role would have seemed unlikely. At the turn of the century some three hundred semi-independent principalities were fighting for identity. Only with the rise of Brandenburg-Prussia through the early decades of the century could one speak of political Germany as an entity with potential world power.

The cultural lore had not been much richer than the political promise. During the German *Aufklärung* Germans found it valid to invent instant cultural history so that they would have a heritage to expound. Not much was on hand. In the literary realm, much was made of Luther's German Bible because of its contributions to the language. In poetry, minor figures like Hans Sachs had to be blown all out of proportion to their actual significance in order to provide Germany with an ancestral past.

When the Enlightenment did come, Germany was influenced somewhat by British thought – Deism having some influence – and many early German trends reflected movements in France, as in the case of correspondence between Frederick the Great and Voltaire. Before long, German thought became self-conscious and more provincial. The German Enlightenment, using raw materials out of the German Protestant past, tended to be more theological and in its own way more Christian than was the French version.

From Gottfried Leibnitz to Gotthold Lessing, German philosophers reverted to theological themes. Atheism was present but rare, cherished as it was by eccentric figures. The main leaders devoted themselves to inclusive theological systems that had room for God, for divine purpose, for reminiscence of Christian themes but with less accent on the particularity of revelation. After these eighteenth-century beginnings, Germany was intellectually ready for its great flowering in the nineteenth century.

That the German territories, heartland of the Holy Roman Empire, should also become the host culture for anti-Christian ideologies seems startling. Germany had experienced a quaking in the sixteenth century under Luther and with the Protestant Reformation, but the disputes of that time had been corralled congenially within historic Christian limits. The Reformation had secularizing effects, but these were not the intention of either party. That modern atheism and other attempts at utterly secular expression should have so many roots in Germany seems to be a departure from that nation's tradition.

Just before the Modern Schism, Germany saw a period of rebuilding and renewal. The *Erweckungsbewegung* took many forms. Throughout the first half of the century there were revivals of the kind of Pietism Germans had known a century and a half earlier in the era of Philip Jakob Spener and August Hermann Francke. These revivals had some similarity to the Wesleyan movement in England. They centred in recovery of Bible-reading, organization of prayer cells, reform of liturgy and worship, personal piety, family devotion, and accent on personal vices and virtues. Social reform was to be undertaken only within the carefully determined limits of the order established by 'the powers that be'.

This awakening reached a political highwater mark in 1817, when the civil authorities imposed a Prussian Union on German Lutheran and Reformed parties. Friedrich Wilhelm III was something of a liturgical dilettante and theological dabbler. His union provided him with an outlet of personal expression and seemed to be politically advantageous as an encouragement to religious unity in those territories which were struggling to become prime in Germany.

Many Protestants went along with his desires, and the churches under his influence knew new favour and power. Unfortunately for the independence of the church, the basis of the Union simply reinforced the centuries-old servility of the German church leadership to the civil power. The Prussian Union tended to keep the clergy in a kind of lower-echelon civil service status.

The Union provided at least a negative base for the stimulation of revival, for numbers of independent church reform movements grew up because of it. Thus in 1817 a party of German Lutherans, setting out to celebrate the tercentenary of the Reformation under the leadership of Claus Harms, saw the flowering of a churchly revival. Under Harms and other conservatives this revival took on less of a pietist and more of a confessional tone. That is, German Lutherans began to re-explore their Biblical and Reformation traditions, particularly in the sixteenth-century confessional writings which had defined the doctrines and character of the Church. The thought world of the new century differed vastly from that of the Reformation, but the new leaders wanted to measure church life in their own time of upheaval by these norms and standards. A recall and recovery of Reformation era hymns and liturgies accompanied this return.

Reformed Protestantism and non-German Lutheranism participated in a kind of revival across Western Europe in the first half-century. Wherever one turns, there is evidence of activity. In the Netherlands, Abraham Kuyper joined others in leading a revival of Calvinist traditions. In Denmark, Nicolai Grundtvig and Peter Kierkegaard; in Norway, Hans Niels Hauge and Gisle Johnson; in Switzerland, Alexander Vinet; in France, the Monod brothers encouraged vital piety, missionary activities, and the recovery of churchly tradition.

During these decades, continental Protestants were also taking part in world-wide missionary activities. They had pioneered in the Pietist era, having sent missionaries to India. In the nineteenth century they never became a match for Anglo-American evangelicals, whose theological energies were being given an outlet in the time of the expansion of capitalist nations. But there was much recovery of missionary responsibility. Some societies were organized, such as those under the pioneering Wilhelm Loehe, for the nurture of North American German daughter churches. Most of the societies, however, looked beyond the daughters to the heathen world.

In the same years continental Protestantism saw the rise of Bible, Tract, and religious education societies. Under men like Johann Wichern there were efforts at alleviating the conditions created by social change in the budding industrial revolution. Wichern's Rauhes Haus provided a home for young people who were seen as the human off-scourings of social change. German evangelicals were often devoted to the urban poor, delinquents, widows, and orphans, offering hope of heaven and some sympathy with and surcease from misery. They worked as reformers in the areas of intemperance, prostitution, and other personal vices. Like their evangelical contemporaries in England and America, they were essentially conservative and engaged very little in fundamental reworking of the larger society. They accented personal piety and individual salvation, leaving men to their own devices to interpret the new world around them.

Without an understanding of the extent and the limits of these awakenings, it is difficult to see how the Churches could have survived to provide one side for the Modern Schism. These intra-Church experiments can be read as the Protestant version of an alternative to the old Catholic Christendom. Like the French and German Catholics, many of them were even ready to look back to the middle ages of Catholic synthesis as an ideal model. That low-church Protestants could have found these 'Catholic' forms congenial is a sign of their ingenuity and hunger for a spiritual unity. Many of them would have agreed with Novalis, no Protestant himself, that the new age was at war with the old, that revolutions and commerce were spiritually devastating: 'This great inner schism . . . was a remarkable indication of the harmfulness of culture at a certain stage.'[11] The nineteenth century was to remain that harmful culture for them.

The fact that Germany had been the seat of the Holy Roman Empire lent some plausibility to the dream. In Christendom there had been an organizing centre for all of life – legal, military, theological æsthetic, popular – on which one could now build again, Protestant style. Gottfried Leibnitz, more than a century earlier, had undertaken correspondence with the great French Catholic preacher and historian, Jacques Benigne Bossuet, Bishop of Meaux, to propose an Enlightened base for Catholic-Protestant, French-German reunion to advance the cause of a united Europe and a kind of Christian recovery.

Yet the dreams of restoring medieval unity in the industrial and nationalist age were to be denied. Germany and France could not and did not get together, as the war of 1870-71 made clear. Protestants and Catholics drew together not at all in the century. Germany's imperial dreams were reduced to a nationalism that turned ugly. Germany was territorially hemmed in. Not everyone responded to the call for Christian awakening. And many Christians had inherited from the Enlightenment something which haunted them like a metaphysical sickness. They wanted an encompassing answer to everything, an all-embracing confirmation of the Absolute. As heirs of a particular, historical, conditioned revelation, the Christians among them tried to relate the historical to the Absolute. Unable to bring the two together, many of them turned utterly secular; others retreated into Christian orthodoxy; still others lived in the agony of the schism. Friedrich Heinrich Jacobi spoke for many gifted people in 1817 when he wrote: 'I . . . am a heathen in my reason and a Christian with my whole heart; I swim between two bodies of water which will not unite so that together they can hold me up, but while the one continuously holds me, the other is constantly letting me sink.'[12]

Such inner tension has often been productive of high art, philosophy, and theology, and this was the case in Germany. Since that time until the present many of the more problematic and promising currents of philosophy and theology have issued from German universities. Early in the century, there were good reasons for this: philosophy and theology were given honoured places in the universities. But theology, the queen of sciences, became less and less the organizing centre of studies. The new universities like the one at Göttingen had been harbingers of this. Germans were to become obsessed with *Naturwissenschaft*, the development of natural sciences, the scientific method, and positivism.

These trends, while they circumscribed the spheres of German philosophers and theologians, did not stunt their creative efforts.

AMBITIOUS THEOLOGY, RELENTLESS ENEMIES

In German theology we see the most ambitious effort anywhere to bridge the developing Modern Schism. Viewing these efforts, it has often seemed to me that later generations of religious believers hardly merit the right to stand in judgment on that part of the nineteenth-century Church for its failure to experiment. While many merely capitulated or surrendered to modernity in its then current forms, the more inventive tried almost everything and their failures tended to run in the damned-if-they-do-damned-if-they-don't category.

Therefore, when a late twentieth-century theologian suggests that all would be well with the Church if it adapted to modernity, understood the *Zeitgeist*, became relevant to the dynamisms of contemporary life, and thought in the patterns of its environment, he may be speaking without awareness of the precedents set during the years of the Modern Schism. Not that the precedent must be determining for the future; it only announces to the breathless discoverers of the principle of relevance: it has been tried.

When Hegelianism was the philosophical mode, few outpaced the Protestants in their devotion to this way of thinking. When neo-Kantian thought-forms predominated, the Protestants again pioneered in the effort to relate these to their disciplines. The Germans tried evolutionary developmentalism, scientific positivism, pure reason, the critique of pure reason, romantic poetry – anything that might help them articulate a meaningful faith for their day. They knew many successes, and modern theology draws on these. But they did not serve to rally the people, who were turning to ideologies of conservatism and liberalism, socialism and nationalism, scientism and historicism – often with a religious fervour. If one wants to fault the theologians, one might concentrate on their almost eerie isolation from the practical concerns of the new industrial workers, the urban poor, and other victims of change in Germany. The theologians concentrated almost all their energies on one of the two great obstacles to faith in their time: they neglected the close-at-hand agonies of interpreting the dislocations industrialism brought. They turned to what might be called the crisis of historical consciousness, out of which crisis many systems were born which *have* addressed the dislocated and the alienated themselves.

This crisis is often summarized under the term *Historismus*, a word coined for the era but one which has been filled with so many kinds of content that it is almost useless today. The question had only been anticipated in the eighteenth-century Enlightenment. It dominated in the new century. Science told men that everything always changes. Romanticism stressed fluidity and relativism. Everything was to be understood in context, in environment. Much later, after he had devoted his whole career to the problem, Ernst Troeltsch commented on what had troubled men for almost a century. He discovered that 'the historical studies which had so largely formed me, and the theology and philosophy in which I was now immersed, stood in sharp opposition, indeed even in conflict, with one another'. His schism in the soul was comparable to that of others: 'I was confronted, upon the one hand, with the perpetual flux of the historian's data, and the distrustful attitude of the historical critic towards conventional traditions.'[13]

The crisis of historical consciousness swept all the disciplines – it was not the private preserve of historians on the one hand and philosopher-theologians on the other. The intellectual version of the Modern Schism can be almost entirely capsuled in this problem. Many, when they saw the relativity and conditionedness of historical Christian claims in the flux of history (or in relation to the Absolute), saw their faith disintegrate and found it necessary to attack the remaining faithful as ignorant or malevolent. On the other side, many men of simple faith tried to harden the data of Christian history into new 'fundamentals' and to affirm them no matter what inquiry concerning them revealed, refusing to reason about their faith. The theologians tried to overcome the gap between the two and to increase communication, to effect synthesis.

The men of the Enlightenment, no less than their critical successors like Søren Kierkegaard, asked it this way: how can eternal and absolute truth or ultimate values be dependent upon a historical event or decision based on a cluster of such events? And what happens to these ultimate issues when those events evaporate in the face of later scientific inquiry? (It was for this reason that the Higher Biblical Criticism, as it came to be known, was decried as a threat to the faith by religious conservatives.)

The German thinkers began to do what their Enlightened fathers had set out to do before them; but now they brought the inquiry into church, as it were. They asked critical questions of biblical literature, of historical knowledge of Jesus Christ, of traditions of the Church, and especially of miracles and evidences of the supernatural. They saw some falsehoods in Christianity and some truths in other religions and in the inquiries of the non-religious.

Two main lines of inquiry seemed open to them. In the Hegelian lineage, some tended to say: no matter. No historical moment is absolute or ultimate. Christianity never was or at least never should have been about this question. All moments are parts of stages in which the Absolute Spirit is struggling towards liberation.

Thus in the work of the pioneer but sophisticated historian of dogma, Ferdinand Christian Baur, the solitary figure of Jesus was to receive less attention than he had in the individualist's or pietist's view of the salvation drama. Following the Hegelians in this respect, men who were more interested in political than in individual history, Baur placed Jesus in a movement. He had grown out of the Hebraic-Semitic world, to be countered by Paul, who brought along some Greco-Roman reflection. Out of these partly conflicting forces came the Catholic Church, a quite different product from the original Apostolic Church. But it, too, was not the final entity and was constantly conditioned by flux and change.

Such reasoning and research fitted in well with Hegelian thought (though Baur did not wish to be thought of as a simple Hegelian) but was unsettling to the German Protestant faithful. All historical bases for faith seemed to vanish along the way. Where was there ground on which to stand, a rock to place one's foot in a time of devastating change? On what could a man firmly base his ultimate commitments?

Another line of approach to the crisis of historical consciousness can be associated with the neo-Kantians, those who were not directly dependent upon the thought of Immanuel Kant in a complete and formal sense but who were inspired by his suggestion that one could not have direct knowledge of the noumenal but only of the phenomenal. This anti-metaphysical bent of thought, almost a direct opposite to Hegelianism, fit in well with the developing scientific interests of Germans and provided a new charter for research in theology.

Theologians in this lineage, like Albrecht Ritschl, engaged in what they thought was dispassionate research into the life of Jesus and the question of Christian origins and tradition. In some ways their work looked slightly more conservative than the Hegelians' line had been, for they had to show respect to revelation and tradition. These formed the subject-matter of their research and they were to be less speculative, to bring fewer presuppositions. But they, too, had to smuggle in a principle by which to explain their devotion to Christianity. Did their findings, for example, really prove that Jesus was a more fitting object of devotion than other heroes? Did he objectively stand out above all other relativities of history? Here Ritschlians imported their equivalent to a metaphysical norm. They converged on a *Werturteil*, a value-judgment in theology, one ordinarily derived from a faith commitment or personal taste. This their scornful enemies eagerly pointed out to them.

Both approaches were directed to the authentic problem. Both left Protestantism vulnerable. From the Hegelian left wing came a group of philosophers who went further than Baur and his colleagues and came to oppose the faith. From the neo-Kantian side came positivist researchers who no longer shared the Christian value judgment and who felt that they could prove that there were no objective and demonstrable reasons in history for men to elevate Christ and the Christian tradition above other heroes and value-systems. Out of the Hegelian line was to come the proclamation of the death of God; out of the neo-Kantian heritage came the observation of the ordinariness of Jesus. Both were intended to be utterly secular.

Since the problem of the death of God has come to symbolize utter secularity in subsequent theology, it deserves more inquiry. Nowhere else was its root so clearly to be defined as in the Hegelian transformation. F. C. Baur, the father of modern church history and of the critical school, said: 'No single moment is to be absolutized or negated.' With these words he revealed his identification with the central German metaphysical affirmations of his day. For Germans, historical consciousness always meant the attempt of the Absolute Spirit to come to progressive realization and freedom. History as a whole, and not Jesus or the Christian tradition, became the bearer of revelation in Baur's

'Tübingen School'.

If Baur somehow kept his 'critical cold water bath', as a shocked student later spoke of it, within the Christian orbit, his successors did not. Their careers took them on the strange line that can be drawn from Hegel to Marx or from Hegel to Nietzsche. To some students, modern atheism begins with Hegel and the Modern Schism would then centre in him. In his desire to do religion a favour by locating it not in the accidents of history but in the whole of history and, beyond this, in the securities of Absolute Idea or Absolute Spirit, he established a basis for successors to see the evaporation of historical religion and revelation: Scripture, incarnation, the crucifixion and death of Jesus, the tradition of the Church.

After Baur the man who most applied Hegelian approaches to biblical materials was the much more radical David Friedrich Strauss. Strauss' *Life of Jesus* was notorious in Germany in 1835 and was, through George Eliot's translation, a chief transmitter of German shock-waves to England and the United States after 1846. It was a foreboding sign of the depth of the Modern Schism in Germany, comparable to Renan's life of Jesus later in France. The book is not well-written and may not have been much read; but its main point was easily summarized and wide sectors of the public knew the gist of the argument.

Strauss did not write a life of Jesus so much as an essay on the near impossibility of doing so. Since the whole of history is the bearer of revelation, Jesus was an isolated figure and did not concern Strauss too much. In Jesus, rather, the whole race suffered; in him the whole race died. For Strauss, myth became a fundamental category and miracles disappeared. The attempt to find the essential or real Jesus enshrouded at the core of the early Christian records was complicated by the supernatural shroud thrown over him. Strauss' conclusion was: 'mankind is the incarnate God'.

With this turn of thought, he contributed greatly to the suggestion that theology is merely and really anthropology and that when men speak of divine themes they are merely exaggerating human ones. Strauss asked himself early on, 'Are we still Christians?', and had to give a negative answer. An unlovable personality with embarrassing conclusions, he caused the Hegelian reputation to decline in the German universities and by the mid-1850s the neo-Kantians came into prominence. The Ritschlians had preferred status. Strauss went on to pursue an independent career and in 1864 wrote a sadly compromising life of Jesus 'for the German people'; here was a book full of bourgeois values, one which caused many to question the sincerity of the younger Strauss and his radical book.

With Strauss, German religious thought was well on its way past Orthodoxy and Enlightenment, past Absolute Spirit and myth – to the edge of the grave of God. Men who were styled the Young Hegelians or the Hegelian Left, anything but conventional followers of their master, eventually 'turned him on his head' as Marx put it, applying his dialectic not to the spiritual but to the material world.

After Strauss, Bruno Bauer became convinced that behind the myth there had been no substantial historical Jesus at all; Jesus was only 'the working hypothesis of God's character'. He spoke of Strauss, the old radical, as a 'Hengstenberg of criticism', Hengstenberg having been the most intransigent notable in Protestantism's conservative citadels.

Ludwig Feuerbach, next in line, explored the whole history and tradition of the faith and worked in a study of Protestant origins, concentrating on Luther. 'Feuerbach was Hegel's fate', wrote enemies of the school. Considered by many to be a mediocre thinker and not a first-rate philosophical mind, Feuerbach was more successful than anyone else at posing the questions raised by the crisis of historical consciousness and, along the way, he turned not only on Christianity but also on Hegelianism. A father and founder of modern atheism, he anticipated Marx, Nietzsche, and Freud in their belief that religion depended upon illusion.

Feuerbach overtly turned theology into anthropology as part of his thesis. He was fascinated with provocative statements like Luther's to the effect that faith was the creator of divinity in man, or again, 'Glaubst du, so hast du': as you believe, so you have. The object of faith disintegrated; it had been an illusion, a projection, a wish-fulfilment. Man written in capital letters was translated into God. Feuerbach moved further towards materialism: 'Man ist was er isst': man is what he eats. He 'denies more to God and accords more to himself'. This is the movement of history.

Max Stirner called this a 'devout atheism', devoted to the shell of Christian philosophy, still too content to leave the world as he found it. In *The Ego and Its Own*, in 1845, Stirner spoke in Comtean terms of Humanity or Society as the new preoccupation: 'Society . . . is a new master, a new spook, a new "supreme being", which "takes us into its service and allegiance".'[14] But Stirner went further than Comte in seeking liberation from the impulse to cast a religious glow over history and society; people were still 'imprisoned in the religious principle' in their quest for a sacral alternative to Christendom.

Karl Marx spotted the theological residue in Feuerbach, too. This is why in his theses on Feuerbach Marx accused the theologically-minded philosopher of being only a philosopher who interprets the world and not a man who changes it. Despite his 'world shattering phrases', Feuerbach worked with reason and not with passion. For Marx, he was therefore almost as useless to the cause of social change as the Christians were. From the socialist point of view he did live at a half-way house. But from the viewpoint of Christian orthodoxy and the historic foundations of Western culture, he was a major agent of the Modern Schism, a proclaimer of the death of God and the irrelevance of the Church, a shaker of the old and a shaper of the new, not merely of Hegel's fate but of an era of German theology as well.

Marx, who had been critical of Bauer and who favoured Feuerbach at first for his materialism, later polished his critical tools on Feuerbach. The theologian-philosopher had not succeeded in removing the conditions which led to the birth of religion. Marx wanted to improve on that. Materialism was to prevail; Max Stirner shocked the idealists by denying even the essence of man. Later, but definitely in this lineage, was Friedrich Nietzsche, prophet of the death of God, agent of utter secularity, articulator of life on one side of the Modern Schism.

That all this could happen in several decades in the orbit of German thought, in the hands of sons of the parsonage and former seminarians, suggests something of the depth of the crisis of historical consciousness and the dis-ease of the German metaphysical tradition. While it was true that the ideological assault on Christianity was largely confined to universities, salons, and *élite* circles, here, clearly, was part of the upheaval or 'fault' in thought which helped produce the Modern Schism.

Other forms of change have had a more numbing impact on Christian programmes and ideas in the modern world, but in the realm of metaphysical atheism, few new issues have been posed since that time. The social transformations of both Marxian and Nietzschean thought in the twentieth century do not require documentation here. In these years, some of the most pitiless rivals of Christianity were born.

The Ritschlians remained more respectable, but they also revealed for all to see the new difficulties of dealing with the Christian sources. 'What is God worth for man?', asked these value-oriented Ritschlians, moralistic as men inspired by Kant have often been. The devotional and liturgical heritage meant less than ethics. 'Where I find mystery I say nothing about it', claimed Ritschl. He moved away from metaphysics and metahistory, helping to provide a theology which could cause men to build or bring in the Kingdom of God. Out of this school grew the liberal heritage which helped German theology buy time and shape the lives of many for the rest of the nineteenth century and down to World War I, when that tradition revealed its poverty and was supplanted by radical new theologies of crisis and of the Word.

In the mid-nineteenth century not a German, but the lonely Danish prophet Søren Kierkegaard, best saw what happened. He looked out on the terrain of Christendom and saw its demise. Luther, he said, had needed ninety-five theses; he would have only one. Christianity does not exist. He attacked the 'system' of Hegel. Like many a solitary seer, this critic of cultural accommodationism (which Ritschlianism became) had little to prescribe to take the place of Christendom. He called for radical discipleship of Jesus. If he had nothing of a social policy to offer, this was in part because he wanted to be the 'corrective against the age'. For him, Jesus was central to history but yet he did not somehow really belong, for he bore a paradoxical relationship to any age.

Kierkegaard in his own way prophesied the death of God and announced the Modern Schism: 'People will soon see how *I* am the one who understood the age.' He was in many ways the opposite of Marx, aware as he was of Marx's insights into the character of labour and capital. Marx, in turn, could have dismissed Kierkegaard as another of those mere interpreters. But he remains the

supremely gifted artist who discerned and chronicled the end of
Christendom behind the façade of the surviving churches.

During the most creative theological period since the Protestant
Reformation and right under the eyes of its agents, the tradition
of modern unbelief and atheism emerged and Christians were
powerless to thwart it.

THE WORLD THAT DEMANDED INTERPRETATION

Those who battled for the mind of Western Europeans from the
narrowing confines of theological faculties and the insulated
studies of universities knew that the struggle was not confined to
the academy. For most people the direct impact of modernity
came in the areas of daily life, areas that had to do with employ-
ment, hunger, the growth of cities, the environment of the home,
disease, pleasures, social affairs, and politics. In those realms the
Modern Schism also was exposed.

That schism coincided with the rise of industrial life on the
continent. The industrial revolution was slower to come to Germany than to England. The two major cities were Berlin, which
grew 110 per cent between 1819 and 1846 and Vienna, which
grew 81 per cent at the same time. Cheap labour came to the cities
and *then* came industrial development. By 1846 in Prussia only
12·5 per cent of the workers were in factories. Weaving was the
first work to be industrialized on a large scale. The railroads came
in 1835 and by 1850 Germany had the largest railroad on the
continent. Population was growing: in three decades the figure of
22,700,000 in 1815 had increased by 38·5 per cent.

These growing urban working masses were anything but ready
for Marxian analysis, and those who have read Marx's writings
about the German proletariat of the time have to qualify his
vision by a study of their actual circumstances. They did not turn
to liberal reformers but to the prince, who was regarded as a kind
of a father to them, in an age with a residual paternalistic spirit.
Not until 1848 did the workers really take part in rebellion and
even then they did so not in response to social doctrine but more
directly because of the urgency of hunger and economic demands.
For a time, men like Marx and Friedrich Engels found themselves
more at home in London and Paris than in Germany.

Few were concerned when Marx's *Rheinische Zeitung* was closed down in 1843 and five years later the *Manifesto of the Communist Party* went almost unnoticed. The revolution of that year was not socialist in inspiration or outcome. The socialists were the weakest of all opposition parties. Workers sought the favour of the middle classes more than they enjoyed the (to them) degrading classification of alienated artisans. Why is it that a century later we look back on the Marxian interpreters of the economic order and see so much potency in their analysis?

They were both off target and on. Off target: they acted like reporters, discussing the presence of a discontented proletariat that was on the point of uniting under their banner. It did not. On target: the discontented masses were there, but were temporarily seeking other refuges and outlets. They did their own attacking of the industrial order, often by waging war on factories and machines. What Marx brought to the German proletariat was not political organization but an analysis of some of the effects of the industrial era, a set of doctrines that when tied to military regimes later was the basis for twentieth-century revolutions – and a full-blown attack on the vestiges of Christendom in the industrial era.

The Marxians saw that a new principle was applicable in the economic order of Western Europe and eventually everywhere. Max Weber called it *Rationalität*, which went along with the principle of specialization and differentiation of roles and functions. 'Rationality' meant more interdependence of parts, persons, and places, for their utility inside a locked-up system. Thus industrialism came to be centripetal and magnetic, demanding all the energies of a social and cultural order. God, Church, and Christian culture had been related to the various parts of the earlier culture. Now they were beginning to be excluded from the whole of the new. God seemed to be superfluous; the Church abandoned the people who most needed means of integrating their new cosmos.

The familiar reckoning of industrial-urban change points to the despair, the lack of co-ordinated lives, the absence of roots, the passion for escape, the alienation that afflicted workers and affected all people who shared utilitarian parts in the industrial whole, the System.

It was the system that brought modernity to the common people.

They did not know where to locate God. They needed Sunday for refuge from duty. The squalid circumstances in which those drawn out of necessity to urban slums lived allowed for no possibility of intimacy, privacy, and nurture – the requisites for Christian life which their fathers' pastors had preached about in villages. The person to person relations of their old communities and parishes were impossible in parishes the size of Berlin's St Georg's (80,000 parishioners), or St Sophie's (over 50,000) in the 1860s. And the romantic discussions about mutuality sound bizarre when applied to parishes of the 1880s, with their souls numbering well over 100,000! The Protestant clergy did not even try to discuss the implications of these circumstances in positive terms. Like a General Superintendent, Pastor Carl Büchsel, who had observed the despair of rural people who were turned out from tenant relationships, they also surveyed the cities and complained that the people had lost all sense of sin and lived and worked in bestial conditions. But before the 1860s not a single Protestant clergyman effectively took part in interpreting the labour movement.

One malcontent clergyman in a novel parodied the situation: 'The men must obey; work hard, learn as little as possible, be pious and vote conservative.'[15] The novel's author knew of Lutheranism's studied attachment to quietism in politics, its authoritarian defence of the status quo. When a few religiously motivated radicals began to appear on the scene around the time of the Revolution of 1848, they had to shop elsewhere for their visions. Thus the spirited and almost anarchic Wilhelm Weitling improvized an approach that had more in common with Left Wing reformers of the sixteenth century than with anything in the established churches of his own time. By the time of August Bebel and Wilhelm Liebknecht, German labour began to organize on non-Christian and sometimes anti-Christian Marxist lines in 1863 and 1864. They were not orthodox Marxists, and Marx had little use for the partly effective organizers like Ferdinand Lassalle, who was also anti-Christian and materialist. All of these pioneers had difficulty with workers, who were not ready to turn their backs entirely on Christianity. But labourers' attachment became increasingly marginal and they took on ways of life that made them look like 'unconscious secularists'. In 1867 in industrialized Berlin only 2 per cent of the Protestants were to be found at worship, and the industrial areas helped bring about the low figure.

Through these decades Karl Marx perceived the failure of Christianity to change the conditions or of its theology to understand them. Out of his perception grew not a successful programme for organizing labour – that came later and elsewhere. Rather, from this time we date the birth of his doctrines which have survived as persistent rivals to those of Christianity.

Marx's attack was knowing and devastating. Those who do not know the metaphysical quest in Germany's social situation of the 1840s will fail to understand why the Young Hegelians and why Engels and Marx concentrated so much energy on theology and Christianity. Why should social thinkers care about the essence of the Church or the possibilities of doing a life of Jesus? These were chosen fields because during the Modern Schism Germany was working itself out of a social and intellectual order which for centuries had been dependent upon these documents, their traditions, and the God to whom they pointed.

Karl Marx argued that the criticism of religion was the root of all criticism. 'Communism,' rather, 'has solved the enigma of history. In one word – I hate all the gods.'[16] It is easy to see why Marx found it necessary to oppose the religion of his day. A new world was being born; new classes came into being; the old order cared only about one of them, Marx's hated bourgeoisie. Religion was used to buy off discontent and to offer eternal rewards to the patient: this was opium.

The churches not only failed to offer a programme for the new classes; rather, they offered the wrong one. Hope in the next life was all that the evangelicals talked about – a perfectly horrendous demonstration to Marx of the churches' ability to exploit misery and hold on to their own security. Had not even Feuerbach shown that religion was wish-projection, anthropology writ large? Hierarchs could manipulate the ignorant and exploit the superstitious. Meanwhile, the conservative clerics were telling the lower classes to be content.

In the history of the West's Christian culture, Marx is one of the chief anti-saints, along with Darwin and Freud and Feuerbach – the giant god-killers of the Modern Schism. What Marx produced was 'a story of salvation told in the language of economics'. From the Jewish and Christian lineages he had taken the view that history had purpose and meaning, but he denied their conventional meta-historical backdrop, their trans-temporal hope.

Messianism he tied to the class struggle; salvation related not to the individual but to the classes, who find fulfilment in their struggles. In a sense, Marxism was a philosophy of history, less than scientific, for it professed to know the outcome of history, to deal with it – not, of course, in detail – as if the future had already occurred. What resulted has been called the first secular religion of the whole world.

While French speculators devised cunning little schemes for cults and utopias, Marx and Engels and their colleagues saw all men as economic beings; all the world as potentially to be industrialized; all industrialization as presenting problems of meaning, value, and power to the proletariat; all proletariats needing liberation; all liberation coming through class struggle; all class struggle as deserving man's ultimate commitment; all men's ultimate commitment confused and compromised if they believe in God. God is dead. Man is free, at least potentially, once he becomes aware of this. Little wonder that Marxism was to become the 'Twentieth Century Islam' as an alternative to Christianity. Karl Marx, little read in his lifetime, in the obscure *Das Kapital* wrote something of a charter for getting out of Christendom, like Augustine's *City of God* had been a charter for its formation.

RELIGIOUS NATIONALISM

If few in Marx's own time followed his programme or read themselves into his prophecy, many turned to a kind of religious nationalism as a surrogate for or successor to Christendom. Nationalism is an international or ecumenical religion having many warring sects. France and Germany were by no means alone in developing it. But the nationalism of especially the new united Germany after 1870 was to have the most fateful consequences in later times. Nationalism's policy differed from that of Communism in Germany in that it did not oppose religion – it made use of it. It did not proclaim the death of God but rejoiced in the life of the living gods and resurrected some of the dead ones. Many Christians, especially Protestants, in traditionalist and authoritarian Germany, were more than ready to permit Christian symbols to take their place in the new interpretation of life.

During the years of the Modern Schism Germany's nationalism no longer remained the romantic, visionary, and still gentle version of the extravagant poets and philosophers who used it to instil a love for a heritage, to provide a basis for identity. The end-product was instead, militarist, xenophobic, and anti-Semitic, laden with religious symbols. Not that some of the earlier scripts by Schleiermacher, Fichte, or Hegel do not sound absurdly jingoist and threatening in retrospect. But read in the context of their own time they were merely patriotic pretentiousnesses, the kinds of exaggerations patriots often indulge in.

Modern nationalism, as one of the persistent rivals which helped create a schism in the culture of the west, transformed the old loyalty shown the *patria* or locality into a pseudoscientific affirmation of blood, soil, language, and artificial tradition. When the new nations turned aggressive and imperial, they demanded evocative symbols and expressive ideologies. Religion could provide these.

The Germans at the beginning of the century were still divided but were converging on a Fatherland which, as a *Weltbürgertum* did not get in others' way and allowed for those of 'impure' blood. The rise of a humourless secular middle class intelligentsia contributed to the more ominous turn. Hegel helped the intellectuals by showing them that the Nation State was 'mind in its substantive rationality', that Europe was 'absolutely the end of history', and that in Germany, its culmination, 'the spiritual is no longer an element foreign to the State'.

Hegel devised a whole mythology of world history in which the Germanic represented a fourth stage. Noble barbarians played a part, as did old Rome and then the Middle Ages, but in the modern age, 'the human spirit has come to stand on its own basis'. 'Humanity beholds its spiritual firmament restored to security.' For Hegel and for German nationalists in general, the Reformation was a great landmark, for 'the pure inwardness of the German nation was the proper soil for the emancipation of the spirit'.[17]

By 1833 in the German Zollverein the Jews were beginning to be made into scapegoats. The metanational myth was changing from the doctrine of nationalism for the sake of the world to one of racial purity against the world; Jews represented the most significant impure minority on the scene. When militarism, a Prussian tendency, was tied to romantic conservative nationalism, Germany was poised to make total demands on its citizens.

Schleiermacher had said: 'it is God who directly assigns to each nationality its definite task on earth and inspires it with a definite spirit in order to glorify Himself through each one in a peculiar manner.'[18] The 'each one' aspect disappears when racialism and military power are fused, as they were in Germany towards 1870. By then, nationalism had become so secularized that even anti-Semitism was to be based no longer on religious ('Christ-killer') themes but became almost purely racial. Pseudoscientific, up-to-date appeals meant more than historic Christian calls to workers and middle-class Germans. By 1880 Wilhelm Marr made this clear: 'There must be no question here of parading religious differences when it is a question of race and when the difference lies in the "blood" . . .'[19] Eugen Dühring, a year later, was prepared to go a step further from religious neutrality to aggression for the secular: 'those who wish to cling to the entire Christian tradition are in no position to turn against Judaism with sufficient force.'[20] (Many who were not atheist asked Germans only to give up the Old Testament.)

The development of nationalism and racism into an autonomous competitor to Christendom is seen most clearly in the career of Paul de Lagarde (Paul Anton Bötticher), the foremost publicist of the nationalist cause during the years of the Modern Schism. Reared in a Christian setting, Lagarde wanted to see a new Christianity – which had as little in common with the historic faith as did Comte's! – to inspire racial and national loyalties. He, unlike Dühring, remained a theist in his outlook, and spoke constantly of the presence of God as a kind of power. He was anti-dogmatic and critical of most inherited Christianity.

As the years passed, Lagarde offered his own ideas as new dogmas, in a national religion or 'religion of the future'.[21] God reveals himself in the will of the nation; he cares about individual persons; these persons can best fulfil themselves in the organism of the nation; through such an involvement, the Kingdom will come to fruition. He did not resurrect the Germanic deities, as his successors were to do; instead, he fused the Christian God with a personal vision, one which minimized Jesus Christ and the Crucifixion. He wrote to Döllinger that to carry out the tasks of the Fatherland was to do the Father's will. 'WE . . . are conspirators of the future', he wrote to Carlyle. In a way, he was right. It is not difficult to make out a case for nationalism having turned out to be the real religion of the modern world, filled as it is with shrines, heresies, foreign devils, gods of battles, ultimate sacrifices, and other religious heritages. And many religious nationalists have, like Lagarde, shrouded their transformation of religion by recalling certain Christian symbols.

In all this, of course, Christians were deprived of their power to judge or rescue people in the context of political society. The clergy were called upon to endorse national life and, in traditionalist Germany, this meant support for the authority as it was. By Bismarck's time, though the Iron Chancellor was personally a Christian, Christianity did not play a part in his concept of the state. He effected a liberation from the Christian concept. The clergy glossed over his omission.

Everywhere in Europe the new nationalism grew. Grundtvig in Denmark devised a 'Folk Church' which would re-explore old Danish myths and fuse them with Christianity. Young Italy, French integral nationalists (as Charles Maurras was to designate his para-Christian movement), imperial British, Americans of Manifest Destiny, all tended to make a God of the state and then to invoke reminiscence of Christianity to justify their creation.

By 1870 modern Italy, Germany, and France had been born – all of them around the idea of a militant integral nationalism which made demands that had once been associated with its rival, traditional religion. And the prophets were silent.

The scene of Church and culture in the 1870s revealed that the Church had survived, and that creative figures remained in it. But if we ask who now takes the initiative in history, who sets the terms for interpreting social and cultural reality, and who changes the world, the action has moved to others. These include authoritarian relics, new liberals, conservative middle classes, socialists, a few Marxists and a multitude of nationalists. The new scientific and industrial *élites* were coming into command. Christians were permitted to minister to the residual private needs of people in parishes.

The sage Jacob Burckhardt looked on the scene from his refuge at Basel University and reported on what he saw with telling accuracy: 'The modern mind aims at a solution of the supreme enigma of life independent of Christianity.' Many modern minds were adrift and thoughtless. Others had thought matters through and, in affirming the death of God, wanted to be utterly secular.

III

Towards Mere Secularity ·
'Everydayishness' in England

We thus surrender to what H. G. Wells called
'everydayishness'.   *H. G. Wood*

A focus on mid-nineteenth-century England needs no defence. The first industrial nation and the most imperial one, it was experiencing a literary rebirth along with extensive constitutional reforms. The religion of this expansive, industrial, and missionary nation also had consequences for world history. Victorian England is remembered for its religiosity; its people are pictured as church-going. Yet the legacy of the middle decades of nineteenth-century England also includes a falling away from church and faith and devotion to new values and approaches to life.

Not many miles of water separate England from the continent. But a study of the Modern Schism there reveals significant differences in the ways it occurred. Twentieth-century Westerners are heirs of the British-style religious shifts as much as they are of the more doctrinaire and ideological changes in France, Germany, or Italy.

Begin with negative references: in England there are few figures comparable to Auguste Comte or Claude Saint-Simon to dream utopian dreams or to devise speculative systems that would replace Christendom. The pedlar of formal 'secular religions' would have met with little favourable reaction. In Great Britain the concerns of the Vatican's Syllabus of Errors in 1864 were regarded as strangely alien; they were given over to the condemnation of imagined heresies. The democracy abhorred by the Vatican seemed to have little to do with the way British people determined their destiny. The modernisms it reacted against had little to do with the genteel theological adjustments that were being made in England. Even England's nationalism was unaccompanied by anti-clerical doctrines as Italy's was in the hands of firebrands like Giuseppe Mazzini and Giuseppe Garibaldi. Few ideologues for fatherland like Johann Gottlieb Fichte or for race like Joseph Gobineau were in sight.

In formal religious thought, nineteenth-century England reveals few metaphysical prophets on the scale of the German Hegelians or neo-Kantians, no religious genius to match a Friedrich Schleier-macher and perhaps no one as competent as Ferdinand Christian Baur or Albrecht Ritschl to tackle the crucial themes of religion and history. Leslie Stephen recalled his Cambridge professor at mid-century as one who accepted 'verbal inspiration', hell, and other ancient teachings, but he 'did not ask too closely in what sense . . . He shut his eyes to the great difficulties or took the answer for granted'.[1]

George Eliot's translation of David Friedrich Strauss' *Life of Jesus* created a stir after 1846, but this resulted more from its sensational exposure of German outlandishness than from its potential threat to the faith of Englishmen. In theological matters, Germany was virtually a code name for dangerous ideas. In Mary Augusta Ward's celebrated novel *Robert Elsmere* the author spoke in typical terms: 'The present collapse of English orthodoxy is due to one cause, as far as I can see, and one cause only – the *invasion of English by German thought*.'[2] The year was 1888, but the sentiment belonged to all the decades after the 1830s.

The radical Young or Left Wing Hegelians would have seemed to be outrageous if not incomprehensible to most of the British. While Karl Marx made his home in England for some time, and while his portrait of man as the economic being had some influence, it is rare to run across British devotees of his view of history and religion in the nineteenth century.

In short, England made its passage quietly, with light ideological accompaniment. If ideology can mean either an integral idea-system or an ideal rationale which serves to explain or to justify a chosen plan of action, the British modes are not well comprehended in the term.

Why are there such differences in the legacies of Victorian England when compared to those from the continent in the same years? Those who indulge in speculation about ethnic make-up and national character have always been ready to attribute all to something that might be called Britishness. In the eyes of many, English-men have long been known for a practical, empirical, cool and steely approach to philosophical or theological matters. Tempera-mentally, they are unflappable. These speculators may be correct. The historian may or may not engage in such theorizing. He is on safer ground if he confines himself to observing that England under-went the experience of what we are calling the Modern Schism in the same years, as part of the same episode, as did its Western European counterparts, but it did so largely without a great credal or ideological clash.

About the fact of change, there need be little question.

CHANGE: SUBTLE BUT DRAMATIC

The England of the 1820s was churchgoing, but it remained so, more or less, in the 1880s. The dramatic decline in church atten-dance – the Britishers' conventional measurement for religious devotion – came somewhat later and endures through the twentieth century. There were few self-named atheists in those decades. Most Englishmen could have responded to interviews by regarding themselves as conventional members of a Christian nation, content with affirming something more than a wan theism and ready at times with a reasonably full-blown Christian orthodoxy. They have left behind libraries full of documents which suggest their pervasive religiousness.

Yet in the same decades, if one looks to see who was successfully beginning to change and interpret the world for the British, one finds a subtle but dramatic alteration. In Frederic Harrison's terms, in 1869, there 'had been abroad a strange consciousness of doubt, instability, and incoherence; and, withal, a secret yearning after certainty and reorganization in thought and in life'. Further, even the time's merits, its 'candour, tolerance, and spirit of inquiry', exaggerated the British consciousness of 'mental anarchy, and gave a strange fascination to anything that promised to end it'.[3] English spokesmen gave the appearance of having been in a shopping mood.

In a time of doubt, yearning, and mental anarchy, many wares were offered. In the earlier part of the century the English had taken up the natural sciences with a fervour that was not to diminish and with a confidence that their findings would square with the scientific world view of the Bible and would be little threat to revealed religion. Late in the century, after Charles Darwin, those who accepted the Biblical accounts often found themselves proclaiming their positive relation to the newly-established scientific order, claiming that they could adapt and relate their faith to that apparently autonomous world view. The collected *Essays and Reviews* by Anglican churchmen in 1860 was the earliest, noblest, and most celebrated attempt to engage in such relating. Others sulked because their contemporaries no longer accepted the old theological explanations of the origin of earth and man.

God and the priests were becoming superfluous in men's scientific inquiries. Latter-day students of life in the century would remember only one or two ecclesiastical figures – John Henry Newman, certainly – as peers of poets, scientists, inventors, and statesmen of the time. Genius seemed to be passing to other realms.

In the earlier decades before industrial growth had brought millions to urban complexes, John Wesley and the evangelicals could minister to what were then thought of as the lower classes, to villagers and farmers, to people on their way through the lower middle classes into relative security. The evangelicals and Methodists offered these people hope of heaven, a defined place in life, a motive for aspiration, and an outlet for emotional and spiritual energies. Late in the century it had become almost a truism to say the industrial workers were no longer in touch with the churches. Inaccurate! snorted some social-minded churchmen. The Church was out of touch with *them*. What is more, it had not lost these labourers: the Church had never found them, never held them. The whole urban labouring class was seen as somehow secularized, its members having turned elsewhere for guidance in organizing and interpreting daily life. A significant exception to this trend existed among some newer Methodist sects and a few other smaller groups eventually knew some successes in ministering to labourers and in helping them fulfil their aspirations. In 1865 Benjamin Jowett noted the failure of the churches to deal with men in work and wages; he said that muscular Christianity 'is gone out' and Anglo-Catholicism had gone aesthetic.

Just as the churches never had been in contact with many of the urban labouring millions, so they gradually ceased to be of significance among most intellectuals and writers By the 1880s, when one comes across an articulate writer moved by explicit Christian faith and devoted to expressions of a Christian vision – someone like the poet Gerard Manley Hopkins – one is moved to express surprise. A rare find! Political, social, and economic thought moved increasingly away from Christian formation. This occurred even though the more celebrated political figures like William Gladstone were highly dedicated churchmen and people of piety.

British political theorists throughout these decades found little occasion to be noisy about opposing Christianity, in part because they largely incorporated its moral codes into their own thought while dropping the transcendent theological contexts. For Jeremy Bentham, John Stuart Mill, and most other theorists, Christianity no longer seemed to matter much when one set out to determine what was basic in the social sphere.

These trends did leave the churches with the ear of many in the middle classes. That they confined themselves to these and continued to have an attraction was no small achievement, for these classes were not insignificant factors in nineteenth-century England. These were the groups which personally benefited from the Industrial Revolution and which expanded significantly because of it. The success of the churches in remaining with them suggests that churches must have been doing something right, even if what they were doing right was tending to alienate them from other groups and to complicate their later life.

The experience of the Modern Schism in England, wherein whole classes of people were no longer in range of hearing the message of the Church, had import far beyond that one small island. British cultural values were being carried into all the world. During the modern industrial development, most world-religion had been relatively quiescent. The great exception had been the activistic and expansive evangelicalism of the Anglo-American nations. The combination of England and America in the early decades of the century during the religious revivals, coupled with the fact that they had the boats and the missionaries and the messianic dreams and the humanitarian impulses – all this lent special importance to what went on as religion and culture were transformed in these nations.

MODERATE CHRISTIANITY, MODERATE ENLIGHTENMENT

Those who know eighteenth-century British history may wonder why one can speak of devastations to faith and to the programmes of the churches in the nineteenth. After all, the eighteenth century was a time of Enlightenment. There had been the Deist challenge. Lacklustre latitudinarianism blighted the churches. People dropped out of ecclesiastical life or took it for granted. The century of Thomas Hobbes, David Hume, or Edward Gibbon certainly posed as much intellectual threat as did the century of Charles Darwin and Thomas Huxley.

Nevertheless, there had been at least a half century of religious recovery, revival, renewal, and awakening after the Enlightenment in England. The churchly excitements repealed or rolled back many of the changes effected by eighteenth-century life in ecclesiastical England. No such comparable rollback occurred after the Modern Schism in the mid-nineteenth century. One may say that the nineteenth century finished off, in a new set of terms, what the eighteenth century had begun. The Wesleyan-Methodist-Pietist-Evangelical experience then was a creative interlude. To understand the character of the nineteenth-century transformations, it is necessary to glance briefly at the nature of British church life as well as what is called the British Enlightenment.

Those unfamiliar with the details of British Christianity have to prepare themselves for encountering vastly different churches from those they have met in Italy, France, or Germany. As on the continent, a strong established church endured, one which somehow seemed to fit into every cranny and nook of British life. At the same time, there was a growing tradition of important dissent and a growing freedom for the expression of religious pluralism. Roman Catholicism after emancipation in 1829 was more free to take on new activities. Presbyterianism, now largely Unitarian, was past its prime. But Baptists, Congregationalists, and most of all Methodists, remained fairly strong until later in the century. This meant that many adherents and faithful in religious circles (about half of those attending church, according to a census in 1851) were not part of the churchly establishment. They were free to criticize the official Church and often did so, when this was to dissent's advantage.

Pluralism, with its competition and variety, while it allowed more options for believers, contributed to the century's religious crises by weakening peoples' confidence in a single (or two-fold, Catholic-Protestant) Christian interpretation of life. At the same time the spread of tolerance and dissent precluded the possibility of the development of strong anti-clericalism as there had been on the continent. The churches of England were moving targets; it was more difficult to mount attacks.

There was another difference: in England the church historian finds less excitement in theology and more interest in the institutional life of the churches. Not that the British were careless or unintelligent about their study of Christian documents and tradition. Rather, they chose to carry on their research in quieter ways. They made less cosmic claims than did their innovating counterparts in Germany, France, and elsewhere in Western Europe.

Some celebrated theological controversies did occur; Frederick Denison Maurice was penalized for his teachings on eternal punishment and Bishop J. W. Colenso got into trouble for his view of Biblical criticism. But these tangles of the 1850s through the 1870s would have been greeted with bored yawns as being tame refinements of positions in the eyes of German and French prophets and experimenters.

The British devoted themselves to Biblical scholarship and their gradually increasing acceptance of Biblical critical viewpoints and findings weakened the sense of assurance many Englishmen had had in the Bible's authority. But British scholars were ordinarily quick to confirm the reality of faith despite problems with the Biblical record. They were less ready to engage in metaphysical speculation about the Absolute Spirit and the Death of God, about big questions for big answers, than were their continental colleagues.

England had also presented Christianity with a more moderate Enlightenment – certainly one less traumatic than France's. That is, the representative British Deists did not find it so necessary to cry in anger against priestcraft – perhaps because so many bishops were near-Deist? – or to demand a crushing of the infamy of the church, its leadership, its doctrines. Some eighteenth-century figures

introduced radical problems for faith; notable among these were
David Hume, through his scepticism about proofs and evidences of
God; Edward Gibbon, because of his unflattering portrayals of
early Christianity, and Thomas Hobbes, in his post-Christian
political philosophy.

These were exceptions. Their kind was answered, to the satisfaction of many Englishmen, by the likes of Bishop Joseph Butler,
Bishop George Berkeley, or even by William Paley.

The moderate Deists themselves, meanwhile, were presenting
shadows of and parallels to many Christian doctrines. They did not
evoke answers as the more radical Hume did. Meanwhile, most of
the answers came by the circumvention of argument, through the
emotional and activist responses of people to the Wesleyans and
the evangelicals.

DIVIDED ROMAN CATHOLICISM

Any design for perpetuating or restoring Christendom, a united
Europe which shared consensus of faith and commonwealth, would
have had to include Roman Catholicism. But the nineteenth
century saw not only few moves towards Protestant-Catholic
rapprochement but also division in the small but reviving Catholic
minority. While Roman Catholicism in England was less noteworthy than in France, its new assertiveness served to complicate
British church life in the nineteenth century. During the years of
the Modern Schism Catholics were experiencing increasingly better
circumstances. Emancipation was effected in 1829; the hierarchy
was re-established in 1850; through all the decades one legal
liability after another was removed.

John Henry Newman, a convert from Anglicanism and by far
the best-known British Catholic of modern times, spoke with a
divided mind about the effects he expected the Catholic revival
to have in England. At times he hoped that England would see a
second spring of Catholic life, its best chance since the troubles
after the sixteenth-century Reformation. But just as often he seemed
to be haunted by the vision of an impending age of unbelief, a vision
nurtured – so said some of those who knew him best – by a nagging
but obscured unbelief in his own soul. The second spring did not
come. An age of unbelief may have been too strong a term to apply

in his own time, but of his two visions, the second is more historically accurate.

The Catholic revival clearly did not progress enough to provide the majority of Englishmen with that single interpretation of all of life which gave coherence to Newman's own. It was unable to head off the Modern Schism or to help determine outcomes for British religion as a whole. The revival was not able to make much progress towards bringing England back to unity or reunion in the Roman fold, even though it was not immediately overwhelmed by growing disaffection, scepticism, or unbelief.

Two great events affected British Roman Catholicism during the years of this study. It met, first, a great influx of Irish workers who provided much of the muscle for factories and mines during the Industrial Revolution. They were the surplus humanity forced into exile by the famines of the 1840s. These newcomers were in many ways an embarrassment to the older Catholic families, to people who had found ways of surviving for two centuries in Protestant England. They came to early statistical predominance in English Catholicism and provided much of the hierarchical leadership. The presence of these Irish-Catholic labourers also meant that in the 1850s and the 1860s English Christianity in the inclusive sense was not wholly out of touch with workers just because the established Anglican Church had difficulty holding their interest. But the influx ended as fast as it began and hopes for sudden growth ended with it. In 1850 England was estimated to be about 5% Roman Catholic and by 1911 it was only 6·5%.

At the other extreme from these nameless and faceless numbers of semi-literate immigrants were notorious converts like Newman himself, who was joined by representative sons of important evangelical families like the Wilberforces and the Mannings. These conversions at mid-century were part of what signified to Newman the chance for a second spring. The flood of converts never became large enough to issue in a reshaping of the Church. But the fact of the conversions alerted all of England to the presence of this restored religious alternative just as it laid bare widespread discontent with the inherited and traditional church.

These two divisive accents were imposed on a third, the old Catholicism which had survived from the Reformation down to emancipation in 1829. The older Catholics were not visible or articulate enough (they had been undercover) and they were generally disinterested in theology. Often moderately wealthy and landed types, they had taken on the protective colouration of their environment and had conspired with their neighbours to live religiously quiet and peaceable lives.

The Catholicism of the immigrant workers derived from Irish religious forms which were themselves rather impoverished by the nineteenth century. And the religion of the Oxford converts, while it gloried in the development of tradition and the organic virtues of an inclusive Catholicism, turned out actually to be the religion of the very few, for an æsthetic and intellectual élite of – one is tempted to call them – delayed romantics. They certainly had an importance beyond their numbers in English religion. But their dream of a new Catholic synthesis for the modern age was not able to catch the imagination of the masses in England.

Divided Catholicism, then, was paralysed in its attempt to unite England in an age of 'mental anarchy'. It helped few overcome their doubts and satisfied the yearnings of not many more.

In 1829 there were about 200,000 Roman Catholics in England; by 1851 this number had grown to over 419,000; but by the end of the century it was clear that Catholic growth had tapered and that Catholicism had not succeeded in keeping England a church-going nation as it still had been at mid-century. Some Catholics had proved that they were capable of showing interest in and being of help to the victims of urban and industrial change. Cardinal Henry Manning sounded like the evangelicals in his policies for ameliorating the conditions of the urban poor. He identified with workers and led them in rallies so often that some critics called him a socialist. Manning knew that private charities were inadequate and he worked for national policies which would meet the fundamental needs of victims of industrial change. But the Mannings provided no new vision and no profound critique; one could speak only with diffidence of a Catholic contribution to British social or political thought in this period.

METHODISM GONE TO SEED

Between the Enlightenment and the Modern Schism, England had undergone a revival of religion rarely if ever matched since the

Reformation or the Puritan era. What were regarded as the bland generalities of Deism and the thin platitudes of latitudinarianism in the older liberal Arminian pulpits were swept aside and replaced by the fervent adherents of the Wesleyan revivals. They antedate this story but demand brief revisitation for the sake of background. Historians have repeatedly recognized the world-historical importance of this religious renewal. John Wesley, shaped by the doctrinal lore of Anglicanism, the moral rigour of the Puritans, the piety of the Moravians, and his own warmed heart became a leader in a movement of reform inside Anglicanism. After early failures in missionary work in Georgia in 1735 he returned to great successes in England.

Wesley and the early Wesleyans, clerical and lay, were successful with many classes of people. They helped produce a genuinely popular movement. Working in rural and village areas they revealed a genius for addressing the hearts of people who were pioneers in the industrial change. They were particularly at home with those who had been uprooted from traditional parishes and relocated in urbanizing centres where they began to make their way into the middle class.

Wesley's was an enthusiastic and inspiring faith, one which motivated and endorsed the kind of work-ethic necessary when great productivity was demanded in England. The Wesleyans struggled long to remain at home in Anglicanism. But eventually there was a parting of the ways and after Wesley's death, by the beginning of the nineteenth century, the movement was hardening into a separate dissenting church that came to look more and more culturally established by the middle of the century.

Historians have long argued whether the hopes of heaven and the organization of life which Methodism provided served as an escape valve at a crucial time. Was it, in short, England's counterpart to and surrogate for the restlessness that on the continent took a more violent form in the French Revolution? Such arguments rest in part on speculation about the might-have-beens in history and perhaps can never be resolved. The fact that they have been so regularly raised is testimony to the dimensions of Methodist success.

A reader may ask: 'Where, then, was Methodism when England needed it in the nineteenth century?' He may ask, that is, if he has an interest in the survival of Christendom and if he recalls that Methodism had had much to offer in its prime. Its mobile pattern gave it a kinetic style that informed the early modern temper. It spoke a language as if by intuition to new classes of newly literate and newly responsible people. Methodism offered an all-embracing vision of life which fused eternal with temporal concerns. It included a programme of action and a way of organizing life which gave people place, purpose, and identity.

Where, then, was Methodism by the 1830s? As Methodist partisans themselves conceded, it had gone to seed. Always Tory in its fundamental outlook, it later hardened into a largely tired and self-seeking denomination under the custodianship of a man called 'Pope' Jabez Bunting, who announced that Methodism hated democracy as it hated sin. The church was later to revive and relate to culture in new ways, but at the crucial stage it had become ossified.

Methodists, of course, were not alone in the turn-of-the-century revival. After the early 1790s the Baptists and Congregationalists began some impressive pioneering in world-wide missions. British dissenters and many Anglicans alike banded together in great missionary societies or worked for humanitarian and benevolent goals. In Anglicanism, a party styling itself Evangelical benefited from the revival.

By the 1820s British Christianity had recovered from many of its losses in the Enlightened-Deist-Arminian era and had become a surprisingly assertive force in the era of England's expansion into all the world. But the Methodists and Evangelicals, along with dissenters, were as divided and distraught as Roman Catholics were. Their spokesmen were unable to provide synthesis for the lives of shopping Englishmen, and initiative in history moved into the hands of others.

THE INDUSTRIAL REVOLUTION

The Modern Schism in England, as elsewhere, was an episode which permitted Christianity to survive but tended to sequester and segregate it from many areas of life. In the British Isles this shift or rearrangement was centred in issues that grew in part out of the scientific and technological developments associated with the Industrial Revolution. Preoccupation with daily life in that era came to dominate in a pattern which may be styled after H. G. Wells' term, 'everydayishness'. It has presented a subsequent century with an alternative to the representative continental changes which had occurred more through ideological fault or shifts. It is no less constitutive of the modern modes of understanding the secular.

Many historians suggest that the take-off in economic growth in England was so sudden that it is indeed appropriate to term the years after the 1760s or the 1770s a time of revolution. It is not necessary here to enter the debates concerning the length of the roots of the industrial process and capitalist expansion in order to contend that the term 'revolution' has little meaning anywhere if it cannot be applied to the changes in the nineteenth century, with its population growth, urban increase, and the great spread of factories and industrial modes of production. These changes affected the outlook of all people so profoundly that they have been compared to those introduced aeons earlier by the discovery of agriculture and the invention of the village.

Men's fundamental views of themselves as productive beings, of the raw materials of their environments, of the size and scope of their globe, of their interaction with others, of the methods of producing and planning, and of their location in a universe of meaning, were all changed by urban and industrial life.

At the beginning of this revolution most people lived in traditional rural and village communities. Only London could have been called a city by modern standards, although Bristol had begun to grow. A mere century later England was a crowded network of great industrial factory cities, which served as magnets to draw or pull people from village and farm.

For some, the Industrial Revolution meant the worship of force and material goods. For others, like Thomas Carlyle, it represented a great muscular expression to be dealt with in agonizing and heroic moral terms. For some it was a threat; the Luddites (c. 1812) tried to destroy the machines. For others it promised opportunity: in no other way could production meet needs. Certainly God in his wisdom had always planned this mode of existence for his creatures!

Reformers, concerned about children and their labour, about

the working conditions of women, about poor men and their forms of alienation and their workers' organizations, saw plenty of need and impetus for doing good. The sudden revolution, they knew, contributed both to the misery and to the enlargement of human possibilities; it transformed some lives but also created psychic damage and left a price in human debris.

For the romantics, the revolution was to be despised; they would take nostalgic refuge in the village England of simple medieval times, when person to person relations had been (at least from the viewpoint of a later century's re-readers' myth) easier to establish. In that myth, a single if implied theological synthesis had united people in their quest for interpretation of life. As far as all that was now concerned, everything was up for grabs, to be debated anew. Carlyle, speaking of the 'total ignorance and mutual heedlessness of . . . poor souls in populous city pent', went on: 'Each passes on quick, transient, regarding not the other or his woes. Each must button himself together, and take no thought (not even for evil) of his neighbour.'[4] Mental anarchy was seen to prevail.

The Industrial Revolution did not by any means immediately or simply sweep away the old piety. While statistics for the earlier period are hard to come by, historians are safe in picturing much of England and especially the middle classes as being church-going throughout most of the century. In fact, when the social revolution seemed to threaten with immorality and atheism, religion and piety for a time became voguish, fashionable, and conventionalized. Moralists were on all hands: 'the fearful state in which we are living', wrote Thomas Arnold, will require 'the greatest triumph over selfishness.'[5] Vice, infidelity, immorality, and even non-conformity had to be countered. Most articulate Englishmen and not only the seemingly crabby evangelicals could unite in such concerns.

PROBLEMS IN THE CHURCHES

Alongside the obvious questions of meaning for people undergoing change, the Industrial Revolution also presented simple ecclesiastical problems. For one thing, the churches were not able to keep up with the growth of cities or to reach many people in huge sectors of these cities. The old, static geographical parish system seemed irrelevant.

Sunday, long set aside for church-going, was threatened and its meaning transformed. Tired miners and factory workers, after the long hours of the long week, needed the day for physical rest and recreation more than for spiritual refreshment. They were disinterested in involving themselves with the churches or, for that matter, with almost any voluntary organization. For the slightly more prosperous, the new inventions made possible escape from Sunday church-going. London cleric T. F. Stooks in 1858 complained that 'in the summer months, when there are Sunday excursion trains . . . there is consequently great temptation, and a very great tendency to desert the church, and to spend the Sunday as a holiday'.[6] As early as 1843, R. Vaughan, in *The Age of Great Cities*, regretted the 'crowds which make their way through the suburbs of our great cities towards the country on the Lord's day, especially in the neighbourhood of London'. They 'convey a most unfavourable impression with regard to the condition of the religious feeling in the case of a large proportion of our people, both in the lower and in the middle classes'.[7]

Theologians and intellectual historians are sometimes tempted to account for profound religious change only because of profound ideological and philosophical change. In the process, they devote themselves to the agnostic books written in mid-century England. They overlook some of the simpler and more obvious causes comprehended in the term 'everydayishness'. People were tired, thoughtless, distracted; old parochial forms had lost their functions and old appeals had lost their drama. Religion offered them little and seemed to be superfluous. They went their own way.

Most of the workers were not religious radicals. They were neither political revolutionaries nor religious revivalists; more often, they simply ignored or were impervious to religious appeals. Horace Mann, agent of the religious census of 1851, saw little antireligion among the workers and called the masses, quite appropriately, 'unconscious Secularists'.

Pews in established churches were rented and the poor were openly unwelcome. Sometimes the more thoughtful devised the thoughtless expedient of providing special services (often at early morning hours) for workers and the poor. The practice was demeaning and unattractive. Some workers claimed that their clothes were too ragged to permit them to attend – which was true. Many complained that what went on in church had nothing to do with their lives. As is often the case, these masses were not particularly articulate, and we have few records on which to base detailed analyses of their reasons for staying away. But stay away they did. Church attendance in labour sectors of cities often ran to one-tenth that in the middle classes.

Dissenting churches were often more adaptive, and were sometimes able to take up the slack as they built inexpensive meeting houses and tried to relate to the life-styles of the people. The bishops of London worked valiantly to build Anglican churches in areas of great growth. But the building of new churches did not mean the filling of them, and church leaders by and large agreed that they were failing among the poor and the industrial workers. Friedrich Engels was not unbiased when, in 1845, he reported that 'the workers are not religious and do not attend church'.[8] But he was not inaccurate. Half a century later his view was corroborated by an informed Reverend A. F. Winnington-Ingram: 'It is not that the Church of God has lost the great towns; it has never had them.'[9]

The mid-century survey provides a statistical glimpse of life in church-going England. On Sunday, March 30, 1851, a census was taken. Making allowances for the inevitable inaccuracies and overlooking the marks of pseudo-precision, we still have some indicators of response. The population in England and Wales was 17,927,609; 7,261,032 were numbered in church; 5,288,294, it was ascertained by mystical arithmetic, could have been there and were not. To contemporary Britishers this percentage in church would look startlingly high but to people in England in 1851 it was shockingly low. Most of all, the poor and the workers who, all agreed, needed religion most, were weakest in attendance. In Bethnal Green, a workers' area, out of a population of 90,193, only 6,024 were at services. Two years later, a Reverend Eliezar Jones, speaking for the Congregationalists, lamented: 'It with us is a matter of deep regret, and not less of astonishment . . . that the artisans and working men of England are so rarely drawn within our circles.' He was not alone. Almost half the people in church on the March day in 1851 had not been attending the established Church of England, which also did poorly with workers.

The 1850s looked like bad years for institutional religion, after the shock of the census, with Methodist schisms, and with general disaffection. A minor revival began, however, around 1854, with the great Baptist preacher Charles H. Spurgeon in London as its focus. Many date the end of this revival around 1865. The Baptists called the years 1860-70 a revival decade and there were sporadic periods of growt after this time. But from 1870 to the turn of the century there was a general decline in church participation.

Statistics of church attendance, church building, and church support are misleading and do not tell the whole story. They do confirm what was already known : that through the middle decades of the century England remained a church-going nation but was losing intellectuals and workers or artisans. For them, God and the church were somehow becoming superfluous and at least the conventionally accepted modes of reaching them, through worship, liturgy, and preaching, had begun to fail.

Evangelical Attempts to Prevent Schism

At the beginning of the period, the evangelicals saw themselves to be singularly equipped to meet the needs of Englishmen in the century, to prevent slippage and schism. They came fresh from some victories in the early decades of the Industrial Revolution and found reasons for self-confidence. Evangelicalism was not so much a formal party as it was an emphasis in the Church of England. Those who held to it straddled low and broad church parties, but they took on distinctive characteristics of their own.

They were missionary-minded, devoted to benevolence and moderate humanitarian reforms. Most of them were relatively conservative politically, having a strong sense of attachment to established order. Their literature reveals them to be dedicated to cultivating homely virtues, accentuating faithfulness at worship, devotion to sermons, personal prayer. At the centre of their theology was response to the redemptive work of Jesus Christ; many of the evangelical hymns celebrate his atonement and the response of the pious heart.

While evangelicalism could tend to be morally rigorous, it was not always severe in relation to all the spheres of life, and many cultured and prosperous people were drawn to it. The merchant families like the Thorntons and the Wilberforces were prominent in evangelical circles. At Clapham, near London, a number of these *élite* families (many of them grandparents of late-Victorian sceptics, it turned out) gathered to practise their way of life and to consort with their kind of company.

The grand humanitarian scheme of these Tory patriots was the abolition of human slavery in the British empire, a course which took their main energies from 1792 to 1833, the year after the death of their chief spokesman, William Wilberforce. With the abolition of slavery, the central impact of evangelicalism on social affairs diminished. Its era had passed, its advocates having been less ready to take on a criticism of close-to-home social conditions. Cynics could say that slavery would have been abolished for partly practical purposes anyhow at about that time, yet there seems to be no question but that men like Wilberforce worked on the conscience of England.

Later evangelical reform energies were devoted not so much to social conditions as to 'vice', to personal problems over which individuals could have direct control. Some concentrated on temperance and abstinence from alcohol; others worked on abolishing the death penalty, prostitution, inhumanity in prisons. The evangelical leaders were opposed to dramatic or violent social change in matters where the fabric of British life itself might be threatened.

The most important of the second generation of public figures in evangelicalism was the Earl of Shaftesbury, Anthony Ashley Cooper (1801-1885). An enemy of ritualism and an ardent evangelical, his career is informative concerning the evangelical mode. He operated within the framework of Conservative Party politics in Parliament after 1826. Opposed to fundamental social reorganization or ideologically based social planning, he worked for improvement of the lot of victims of social change. The Ten Hours' Bill of 1846 and the Factory Act of 1874 bore the stamp of his activity and personality. His conscience directed him to bettering the conditions of chimney sweeps, child labourers, women working in mines. A power in British ecclesiastical politics all his life, he revealed how much could be effected within the conservative context. At the very least, his name must be invoked against those who saw religion only as the opium of the people and its successful adherents as heartless and thoughtless exploiters. But he was a rare and sometimes isolated figure, and his reforms could be enacted without social upheaval.

The Wilberforces, Thorntons, and Coopers regarded poverty as being a permanent and almost predetermined (but often largely deserved) aspect of the human condition. Most of their charities went into tractarian activities for the propagation of the Gospel. 'How beautiful', said Henry Thornton, 'is the order of society . . . when every person adorns the station in which GOD has placed him; when the inferior pays willing honour to the superior; and when the superior is diligently occupied in the duties of his trust . . .'[11]

Charity on the part of evangelicals to the less fortunate was a legitimate mode of approach. But suggestions that the order of society might itself change and that not all should or would remain content with their status, as if thus to fulfil the plan of God, would have run counter to their most cherished belief.

Out of thousands of options, one vignette will illustrate. Marianne Thornton described the baptism of Lucy Thornton early in the century. 'Of course,' she said, 'we have no finery for such occasions, but still the white as snow, full and flowing garments of the child and her Clapham relations were contrasted to a 'little child of the smallest, thinnest kind' covered barely by a wretched coloured old frock and ragged little towel. The parents were apparently so poor and hungry that 'Mr Wilberforce said they all looked savage'.

Marianne was much affected by the striking contrast and 'could hardly forbear weeping while I put a few shillings into the poor woman's hand'. And then, in lines that Karl Marx would have found useful as Document A : 'However, I recollected that to the poor the Gospel is preached and that it is only for a few fleeting days that the difference really exists. May they both be heirs of salvation.' A perfect evangelical punch-line follows immediately. 'In the afternoon about 20 children ate some strawberries under the tulip tree and Mr Venn gave us an animated lecture on the duty of parents.'[12]

The Methodists held generally evangelical views about status and differences in society. Under Jabez Bunting (after 1828 : 'The whole Methodist Conference is buttoned up in a single pair of breeches') the Methodist Conference had settled into bourgeois respectability and self-concern. Not until the 1840s were there signs of new life, and these came as the result of rather ugly divisions and schisms, some of which resulted in permanent new Methodist sects.

While this splitting-up looked harmful to Methodism, it did free some radical groups in that tradition for new identification with society. Thus when British labour was finally free to be organized into unions, much of the leadership came from these smaller Methodist groups. Had more dissenting and evangelical clusters been as successful in ministering to and organizing labour as these few latter-day Wesleyans eventually became, the record of British workers' involvement with religion might have been considerably different.

ANGLICAN ATTEMPTS TO HOLD THINGS TOGETHER

After evangelicalism's prime, two Anglican movements best serve to indicate churchly responses to societal change. They are familiar to all students of nineteenth-century England as The Oxford Movement (or Tractarianism) and Christian Socialism. They reveal vastly different and largely unsuccessful ways of construing and coping with change in the interest of man and the Church.

The Oxford leaders saw themselves as the most plausible advocates for means of retrieving Christendom and preventing a schism in the civilization. They knew the price would be high in intellectual assent and moral energy; they wanted to pay it and asked their contemporaries to join them. They occupy the attention of Anglican historians in the period after the evangelical prime, holding sway from approximately 1833 to 1845.

The saintly John Keble had preached a sermon critical of Parliament for determining episcopal matters in the Anglican Church of Ireland in 1833. His reaction to this 'National Apostasy' drew attention to a group of Oxford scholars and students who were working and yearning for the recovery of the identity of the Church. Theologically often moderate and in many ways personally romantic in outlook, they cherished continuity in the history of the Church and stressed the organic character of its life. Thus they were theoretically poised to provide over-all synthesis for interpreting reality for many Englishmen. Concerned with doctrine and liturgy as bearers of meaning, they created a sensation through their *Tracts for the Times*, tracts critical of a relaxed Church of England and a secular society. The conversion of John Newman to Catholicism in 1845 was a blow to a movement that had often been regarded suspiciously as a half-way house to Romanism, and while the Oxford influence lived on, it never again occupied centre stage.

One might reasonably ask what this minority and slightly snobbish movement has to do with a history of secularization and social change in Western Europe. At first glance it looks like mere retreat or escape into private ecclesiasticism. The Oxfordians were provincial, even in their claims to be catholic, flailing as they did at the evangelicals, the old high, broad and low church parties, at dissent and Roman Catholicism, at the Erastianism that afflicted the Church on one hand or the threat of complete separation of Church and State, which seemed to some people to be the alternative, on the other.

More was at stake, however, than these narrow church battles. The Oxford men properly sensed that the modern experience in an industrial nation was corrosive of the identity of the Church and not merely of individuals in quest of meaning. What hope was there, they asked, if the Church only loses itself by adapting to modernity, adjusting its message, trying to be superficially attractive, blending into the secular order – and in the process no longer remaining a beacon or an arc for lost men and nations? The Church must retain its own integrity, for that is the purpose of the Church and only in that way can it be an instrument through which society and men can be served and saved.

The movement had significant parallels elsewhere, and these might even be called the romantic mode of attempting to head off schism or at least to minister to its victims. Among the parallels were the Mercersburg Movement in the German Reformed Church in America or the High Church party of Bishop John Hobart in American Episcopalianism; the liturgical and confessional revivals in Prussia and Saxony; the Reformed confessional renewals like those under Abraham Kuyper in Holland or the Lutheran versions under men like Nicolai Grundtvig in Denmark. In all these efforts there was a sustained attempt at resisting mere secularization and cheap accommodations to the world as it was. To students in a later period many of the activities appear to have a defensive tinge, yet they did make an appeal to the emotional needs of many people.

The Oxford Movement, for example, helped the British clergy at large in their task of redefining the Church. Its leaders helped make religion somewhat more intellectually (and, through a 'cousin' movement at Cambridge æsthetically) respectable. Some intellectuals who had dismissed the Church as being emotional and cheap took a second look. As a part of the Church catholic, Oxford found its place. As the answer to the problems of society and religion or for its appeal to the English masses of 1840, it was no more than a minor note.

CHRISTIAN SOCIALISM

Christian Socialism, the name given to a numerically small but disproportionately influential movement, was also designed to head off a schism in the culture, to prevent disaffection with the churches, and to understand and serve new clusters of people. Like Tractarianism, the Christian Socialist movement also used some romantic models of the organic life of medieval England in the attempt to effect its purposes. And its purposes, as one leader put it well, were 'to Christianize socialism and to socialize Christianity'.[13]

The socialism of which Frederick Denison Maurice, John Malcolm Ludlow, and Charles Kingsley spoke was a theological ideal. The movement had little in common with secular socialist endeavour. These Anglicans convinced themselves that the plan of God had not been confined to a pure *laissez-faire* society of utter economic competition. Rather, Christian teachings concerning Baptism and the Body of Christ committed people to a society of co-operation and common involvement. The industrial era had both exaggerated the need for such common commitment and provided new opportunities for its expression.

Some of the socialists, like the layman Ludlow, had had occasional contact with Karl Marx and other socialists, and there had also been a minor influence of British visionary socialists like Robert Owen on other religious leaders. But for the most part aggressive Marxist interpreters of history would have dismissed Christian Socialism as opium or distraction for the purposes of buying off discontent. Ludlow himself had said that while it sought to realize itself in the industrial sphere, 'our movement is above all a spiritual movement'.[14]

Christian Socialism came into its prime between 1848 and 1854, years of unrest on the continent. It was designed to be a response to the industrial situation in sometimes doctrinaire theological terms. The movement's most telling impact came in its criticism of those churchly parties which contented themselves with individualistic charities and ameliorative activities but which failed to get at the base of the socio-economic problem. The leaders asked what specifically Christian kinds of action might look like and then tried to effect them. Their institutional experiments and achievements were very few and not very successful. They devised plans for common ownership, co-operatives, and night schools for workers.

Their Working Man's College (London, 1854), their part in the Industrial and Provident Partnership Bill (1852) and the Co-operative for Promoting Working Men's Association were marginal achievements. What went wrong? For one thing, they came on the scene in the 1850s, when England coincidentally was coming into a brief period of relative economic recovery and affluence. Why bother to reorganize society, if what one already had seemed to be working? Second, the mentor of the group, Maurice, was sometimes remote from the day-to-day activities of the movement and his theological accents were obscure even to professional scholars. Little wonder that they lacked popular appeal. For that matter, the whole movement looked too doctrinaire, was too much in the hands of an intellectual *élite*.

Someone today with an interest in seeing vestigial English Christianity address the problems of its age might be tempted to look back at Christian Socialism and confer on it a 'Nice try!' It was short-lived, atypical of the Anglicanism of its day, but innovative and well-intentioned. At least it signifies that some Christians were ready to recognize the need for structural changes in society. Not all were ready to accept the social contract that evolved in the earliest stages of industrialism. They wanted to help bring about changes and were prepared with an embracing vision of life for their adherents. But what had been designed to be catholic turned out to be sectarian, one lost voice among many.

For those who look for limited but delayed outcomes of causes in history, partisans of Christian Socialism could take some comfort from the fact that through the later Guild of St Matthew their influence lived on into the twentieth century, when one British churchman was to aver, 'We are all Christian Socialists now'. The American Social Gospel movement and especially Episcopal social Christianity were also influenced by the mid-century pioneers.

Neither practical politicians nor revolutionaries had occasion to tremble in their presence, but their insight into the needs of their times at least demonstrates that some in the churches were alert. *Contra* the evangelicals who preached contentment with the status of the poor, Maurice, a lonely prophet, raised an exceptional voice. 'Our Church must apply herself to the task of raising the poor into men; she cannot go on . . . treating them merely as poor.'[15] But even Maurice was not able to move beyond the simple organic village models of the irretrievable Middle Ages. In a publishing practice that reveals much about the age, *Church and People*, the monthly paper for the Church Pastoral Aid Society (for 'the maintenance of Curates and Lay-Agents in populous districts') was graced with a cover that portrayed a medieval church in a small village. Maurice would have been at home with that.

The preceding analysis of England may have looked to some to be obsessively concerned with the condition of the new workers, with the static role assigned them by Evangelicals, and their place in a *laissez-faire* and mildly reformist society. Was there an implied Marxist bias built into the obsession and the narrative? Another way to put it: had the churches in England neglected and lost the middle classes but succeeded in winning the allegiance of workers and of helping change society to better their status (with the adherence of the intellectuals and the writers thrown in for good measure) would they have been pronounced successful? Would the secular trend have been aborted, the Modern Schism averted? Hardly.

The concentration on the industrial worker and the urban poor was designed not to permit a later historian to utter condescending judgments on a blundering earlier age. Rather, the interest has been to show how the churches related to new forces on the scene, groups that were seeking voice and power and who were out to achieve them with or without religion.

By the 1830s all could see that churches were capable of attracting members of the aspirant middle classes and people of conformist temperament. Could they serve a class which seemed to have less to offer, a group to whom outreach might mean the alienation of other clusters? Each generation seems to be given to a particular challenge. The American Social Gospel faced the problem of the urban poor. Another generation had to cope with labour's demands to organize; still later, the movement of northern urban blacks had to be faced. The failure of the British with the labouring groups meant, for them as for continental Protestants in the industrial era, that the majority of people in a new age were forced to prove that they were capable of interpreting and changing their world without the interest or participation of the Church.

Everyday life, then, became the testing ground for the churches, most of whom responded with social models, moral programmes, and redemptive schemes appropriate only to a pre-industrial age. The old syntheses no longer commended themselves with power. Initiative was slipping. God seemed to be extraneous to major human concerns. One could concentrate as well on the nineteenth century's new poets, new politicians, new scientists, new theorists, and see the same psychic outcomes, even if not on the same mass scale. And the mass scale is of interest to those concerned with 'everydayishness'.

To the masses, it was not the lonely evangelical, the æsthetic Oxfordian, or the theory-minded Christian Socialist who represented the Church. They looked, rather, at the men in power, at official spokesmen. If there was ever any doubt about the role of the established church in these years, the attitude of the Anglican bishops towards the Reform Bill in 1831 and 1832 should clear the scene and set the stage. The Reform Bill was anything but radical. It enlarged the franchise in industrial cities, but did not really include anyone below the middle class in its scope. The bishops were spotted as being identified with the vested interests. Placards of agitators in the period attacked and derided the bishops. Some were burned in effigy in one of the rare outbursts of raw anti-clericalism. The episcopacy somehow weathered the Reform Bill and learned to live with it. But the Church was scarred because of this typically defensive gesture. By 1833 Thomas Arnold was ready to describe the ecclesiastical scene as it faced the Modern Schism: 'The Church as it now stands, no human power can save.'

THE AUTONOMY OF POLITICAL THEORY

One can observe the progressive secularization at mid-century by following trends in political theory; at the same time, the peculiarly British path to the secular is also laid bare. Marxism was highly unsuccessful throughout the century. The most prominent homegrown socialist, Robert Owen, who had been a relatively successful factory owner in Scotland and a relatively unsuccessful utopian community builder in the United States, mounted an anti-Christian attack. Both for that gaucherie and because of his fanciful and flighty ideology he attracted little following.

The utilitarians were the more representative British social and political thinkers. In Jeremy Bentham and John Stuart Mill one can see the development of an autonomous theory and ethic, one which paralleled and echoed conventional Christian and even evangelical ethics. If these utilitarians are considered to be among the leaders of 'the other side' in the schism in England, their moderation reveals the contrast to continental ideological assaults on religion.

The utilitarians, like the evangelicals, were uncritical of *laissez-faire* economics. They both argued for personal liberty and placed a high premium on individual energy. They were determinedly opposed to the authoritarian tradition in the churches and to much institutional religion as such, but this opposition was quietly expressed and its effect blunted by the Victorian respectability of the ethic.

George Eliot, not a utilitarian but concerned with the quest for a new moral pattern, spoke for many when she recalled her upbringing: 'Evangelicalism had brought into palpable existence and operation . . . that idea of duty, that recognition of something to be lived for beyond the mere satisfaction of self, which is to the moral life what the addition of a great central ganglion is to animal life.'[16] Men could react against Calvin's arbitrary and capricious God without rejecting the old morality. The figure of Jesus as ethical leader survived men of anti-theological bias. One Bentham title was *Not Paul but Jesus*. Even that seems too frontal to be representative. Typically, Bentham, as an early Utilitarian, is remembered as a man of more continental doctrinal outlook, with less impact in England than many of his contemporaries knew.

Whatever he was, he was never fully ex-evangelical. Back in the Wesleyan era, he spoke of an acquaintance as having been 'what I had liked to have been, a methodist, and what I should have been still had I not been what I am'.[17]

The utilitarians thus look like a harmless group of specimens among the options in secularizing English social thought. They advocated quasi-Christian virtues, according to the measures of their times. Middle-class values predominated, and a high premium was placed on property and benevolence. They devised theories for the commonwealth of everydayishness. Except for minor details, and if they could have advocated belief in the now-extraneous Christian God, a Wilberforce or a Thornton could have lived quite comfortably with them.

They are important in this context for they are a typically British emphasis. They reveal how quietly the British made their move from evangelical other-worldly ethics to utilitarian and steadfastly this-worldly concerns. Morality was the great tent under which people could make their move from one camp to another. Leslie Stephen, heir of Clapham and drop-out from Darwinism, could later write: 'I now believe in nothing, to put it shortly; but I do not the less believe in morality . . . I mean to live and die like a gentleman if possible.'[18] The churchmen could regret the destiny of his soul, but could find little fault with the intentions of his life. To a Stephen this demonstrated that God was superfluous in vital human concerns and decisions.

The utilitarians and the moralists were not alone in the field of contention for the future of the commonwealth. More radical were the Chartists, organized after the Reform Bill was seen to have been too limited in 1832. Chartism, much feared by the establishment, did not make a point of militant anti-Christianity. Some leaders even organized Chartist churches as an act of rebellion against the conventional churches' social programme but not necessarily against their God or against the values of religion.

In these realms, too, the British change was made less through ideology (*à la* Owen) than through the quiet daily mundane adjustments to life in an industrial age with its own practical demands and preoccupations. One is tempted to speak in barbarisms and suggest that in England one confronts not secularization but mundanization, not secularity but mundanity.

STRESSES IN THE DARWINIAN AGE

Concentration on mundane life in an industrial age should not be undertaken at the expense of a survey of intellectual or æsthetic realms. Ideas have consequences, and so do poems. Even though these may not have immediate mass effect, they do inform people and they reflect what might have been overlooked in a superficial reading of history. They are bearers of meaning and they deserve scrutiny.

In England the name that comes to mind immediately when religious and cultural change in the nineteenth century is mentioned is Charles Darwin. He is sometimes mistakenly placed with the ideologues, just because he was one of the century's great bearded god-killers, even though his god-killing was at most accidental. His *Origin of the Species* in 1859 is often called the book of the century. It did help usher in a new epoch in religion and in British and Western cultural history.

I am reluctant to overstress that one book or that symbolic moment, being cautious against locating a watershed year or event. But the years around 1859 were full of trauma. A year later, liberal churchmen came up with *Essays and Reviews*, and two years further on the Colenso controversy over the authority and reliability of the Pentateuch was stirring the church people. The picture of Jesus was being changed through the translation of Renan's life of Jesus in 1863 and J. R. Seeley's merely humanistic *Ecce Homo* in 1865. The British Association which in 1860 witnessed the defeat in debate of a Christian bishop who attacked Darwinism, in 1870 explicitly endorsed evolution. True, these years also saw revivals: in 1859 in Ireland, throughout the 1860s among the Baptists, in 1873 under American evangelists Dwight Moody and Ira Sankey. The stakes were being raised by the time Darwin's capstone work, *The Descent of Man*, appeared.

So Darwin's two major works bracket the period of greater than usual formal turmoil. But mild turmoil was constant. In the 1840s, James Anthony Froude recalled: 'All around us, the intellectual lightships had broken from their moorings, and it was then a new and trying experience.'[19] A later generation, he noted, had grown up in 'an open spiritual ocean' and was used to swimming for itself. But his own had found lights drifting, compasses awry, nothing left to steer by except the stars. John Addington Symonds used similar language in the Darwinian age: 'The whole fabric of humanity, within and without, rocking and surging in earthquake throes',[20] was his account of the Modern Schism in direct but dramatic terms. What was chronic in these decades was acute in the Darwinian context. The roots of the change went back decades before 1859. Between 1820 and 1840, when the French and the Germans were playing speculative metaphysical games, the British took up geology and natural sciences in general with a passion. The early geology had been developed under instinctively Christian outlooks and terms. The Bible served as a guidebook to scientific questions and was a measure of many of the answers. An explanation could be found for every contradiction. The Genesis chronology was perceived to be no particular problem to an Adam Sedgwick or William Buckland. After all, God could have built fossils into his creation.

The beginning of the big change might better be dated with the anonymous publication of Robert Chambers' *Vestiges of the Natural History of Creation* in 1844. This popular book embarrassed professional geologists even as it shocked the multitudes because of its implied and its direct attacks on Biblical chronology. During these years theological thought about modes of literary expression in the Bible had been neglected and original thought on the doctrine of creation and the development of the natural order had atrophied or disappeared.

Meanwhile devotion to the natural sciences grew in prestige and attracted the attention an earlier age had devoted to theological pursuits. The change was not all serene and steady. In these years Englishmen devoted themselves to hypnosis and mesmerism, phrenology and astrology; not all were cool, pragmatic scientists. There were fads and fevers on all sides. But behind them all was the sober pursuit of the scientific. At Cambridge the Tripos exams in natural science were initiated in 1851. Theologians like F. J. A. Hort found themselves much at home in the new climate there. The new red-brick universities were built to recognize from the start the primacy of natural sciences and education for industry and technology.

The original conflict, then, came not over the substantive findings of scientists but was rather the result of a change in preoccupations, in a movement from the supernatural to the natural, from the transcendent to the immanent, from revealed religion to positive mundane inquiry. A scientific attitude prevailed over against the religiously dogmatic ones. People accepted something as true if they found it to be true and not because a bishop told them it was. Men became preoccupied with the reality near them, to the neglect of the earlier favoured transcendent order.

During the years between *Vestiges* and the *Origin of the Species* more and more scientists began to lean towards evolutionary views of origins in creation. Sir Charles Lyell had criticized the young-earth-idea people associated with biblical chronology and the idea of the flood described in Genesis. Worst of all, for Christians, Lyell ignored theology, something which was more devastating than had he chosen to attack it. Alfred R. Wallace also anticipated Darwin's *Origin of the Species* in many ways. But it remained for Darwin, the ex-Divinity student, to awaken the world to the degree to which these theories had developed. Not since Newton had British science produced a man of his originality or stature.

A graphic way to look at the change wrought by the Darwinian era might be to picture the furnished mental apartment of a typical thoughtful Englishman of the 1830s and contrast this with that of his son or grandson in the 1870s. In the earlier time, the cosmos would have been young, created in six days six thousand years before; man was sprung from a single pair named Adam and Eve and rescued through the single family of Noah. By the end of the Modern Schism many in the churches would still have believed this, though they may have been defensive or found it necessary to put these beliefs in a pigeon-hole. At the same time many others, Christian or not, lived with an older, larger cosmos; they had a different accounting of the origins of man and the record left by geological events.

Darwin, who consolidated many of the efforts which effected this shattering change, almost incarnates the personal British style through which the Modern Schism occurred. Born in 1809, he had come under Unitarian influences, but his father sent him to Cambridge to be prepared for the Anglican priesthood. There he was at first impressed by William Paley's theodicy. Later he was to leave Cambridge because other interests crowded the humanities and divinity from his mind. From 1831 to 1836 he took the well-remembered voyage of exploration and science investigation on *The Beagle*. For years he worked out theories based on these findings.

When he finally published them, the book caused a sensation. The clash between science and religion came to a focus. The public recalls the least fortunate and by no means most representative of these encounters, when Bishop Samuel Wilberforce, son of the sturdy evangelical, debated with Thomas Huxley, Darwin's gifted interpreter, before the British Association at Oxford in 1860. Wilberforce largely disgraced himself in the eyes of the audience and left a firm impression that the whole clergy was opposed to Darwinism.

Anything but that. Actually, many clergymen had by then begun to adapt to the emerging world view and some even saw in it an enhancement of Christian theological themes. F. J. A. Hort was undisturbed by Darwin's book. Henry Drummond, moderate enough to share a bandstand with the American evangelist Moody, welcomed it. In popular piety the trauma developed. Darwin seemed to be challenging the inspiration and veracity of the Bible – though this bothered relatively few in the more formal theological company. The scriptural account of creation had been challenged. Darwin's views seemed to do less than full justice to the idea of human dignity and the special creation of the human soul.

Cherished British-style views of natural theology and design were being shattered. Newton and Paley were more threatened than was Genesis: they had been more scientifically explicit! But Darwin himself best describes the process through which transformation occurred for him, how he chose sides across the schism in the culture. No rage against deity or polemic against the churches animated him. 'I gradually came to disbelieve in Christianity as a divine revelation.' He went on; 'This Disbelief crept over me at a very slow rate, but was at last complete. The rate was so slow that I felt no distress, and have never since doubted even for a single second that my conclusion was correct.'[21]

These words stand in contrast to the joyful wisdom of the Nietzsches or the anger of the Marxes. Darwin elides into disbelief. Words like 'little by little' and 'bit by bit' are typical of diary entries of those who changed faith or lost faith in Darwin's years. Nor was Darwin eager to supplant the old gods with new deities, cosmic schemes, secular churches, and plans for everyone's lives.

In a quiet way he seemed to fear mental anarchy and yearn to hold on to the old. In his *Autobiography* he was still willing 'to look for a First Cause having an intelligent mind in some degree analogous to that of man; and I deserve to be called a Theist'.[22] He was never an atheist, he said, even in 'my most extreme fluctuations', and preferred the term agnostic, invented by Huxley. But I take his self-description in a letter to be most accurate, most personally satisfying to Darwin, and most descriptive of the way a generation in England made a transition. He was content to live with a theology that was 'a simple muddle'.

Today it is hard to picture the furore such a mild man and such an adaptable theory created. Most Christians have somehow made their peace with evolutionary thought and many are ready to make it the key to understanding all of Christianity. Opposition by Christians had occurred before in the face of scientific discoveries by Galileo, Copernicus, and Kepler. It was to reappear in the case of Freud. But Darwin seemed to be a special case. It was all right to relocate the world and the sun, but to give another account of human development struck too close to home.

People were disoriented, their cosmology had been shattered, along with their confidence in their old Christian mentors and tutors, some of whom now argued among themselves. They may have been confused by what a later generation would call a tyranny of false alternatives between a dying individualistic Christianity and the excitements of a new science. They felt they had to choose, and many of those who did fell on one side or the other of the party lines in the Modern Schism.

The churches somehow survived Darwin, who did not want to be bothered by theological questions or inhibited by clerical interests. In this respect, too, he was more typical of his profession than were Thomas Huxley or the evolutionary social scientist, Herbert Spencer, who occasionally attacked the Church in vehement and polemical fashion. But even Huxley moved no further than what he called agnosticism. These men did not kill God; one might say they left him alone during his natural death agony or they barely looked up to see him disintegrate into the near abstraction of First Cause mists or agnostic myths. It was often the church people who raised the stakes, asserting that if the evolutionists were right, God was dead. But just as many church people adapted and busied themselves with living down one more embarrassment in their past.

Through Spencer, Darwinian ideas were to be applied to the social sciences. In that realm, curiously, evangelicals in both America and England had less difficulty. Ideas about the survival of the fittest, when removed from science to social order, gave little disturbance to those who knew they were fittest and were in pursuit of justification or a rationale.

Meanwhile, British sciences developed on other lines; an empirical and sometimes positivist temper prevailed. Anthropology threatened some, mainly because it relocated and relativized the religious response, to remove the distinctiveness and superiority of Christianity (as James Frazer's *The Golden Bough* was to do for a wide public). In all this, the churches found themselves choosing between adapting and working out new synthesis, at expense to their past hold on truth; of being neglectful of modern science, and living with their own simple muddles; or of becoming defensive, at the risk of becoming cultural eddies away from the main stream. The worst fate they suffered was the most frequent one. They were simply regarded as superfluous, extraneous, dismissible in these realms.

The whole story of the British change can be told with virtually no reference to formal atheism. The term for the workers was more apt: here were unconscious secularists. Huxley's 'agnosticism' was as far as almost anyone went. G. J. Holyoake, unread today but religiously notorious in his own time, caused a minor stir by organizing societies of secularists. And Charles Bradlaugh, late in the century, was the centre of a controversy over whether he could be seated in Parliament because he did not believe in God and therefore would not take an oath. But lively as Holyoake and Bradlaugh are, they remain curiosities and mavericks. Their careers are less revelatory of the British experience than are those of Darwin and the scientists or than are the day to day mundane adaptation of common men to work and leisure in the industrial age.

SPOKESMEN FOR DOUBT

The Modern Schism occurred, then, because whole classes of people in England – labourers, intellectuals, social thinkers, scientists, found God and the churches to be superfluous to their mundane pursuits. Whether the churches could have found a course to prevent the shift in the culture is a question that belongs to speculators and not historians. One could judge that churches might have more successfully related to certain personal needs and social interests of people. But to answer whether the schism itself could have been prevented one would have to make a theological commitment to the truth of the Christian claims, a commitment which belongs to faith and not to history.

The inherited religion, one must simply report, did not provide a scheme for interpreting the cosmos or the social process, though it did live on residually in Victorian personal and family life or in the careers of gifted men like F. D. Maurice or Gerard Manley Hopkins. There was no cosmic battle between Christ and anti-Christ, Church and anti-Church, clerics and anti-clerics, living God and dead God.

If the secular transition was sudden but subtle in England, it did not go unnoticed among the intuitive poets and writers. Sometimes they served as a kind of Greek chorus, celebrating and lamenting the changes. At other times they were themselves protagonists in the drama, themselves expressing the trauma of change. A few of them sometimes sounded like *poseurs*, but at their best they rose above it, as in the well-remembered lines of Matthew Arnold:

> And we are here as on a darkling plain
> Swept with confused alarms of struggle and flight,
> Where ignorant armies clash by night.

Whereas in America the literary figures were to welcome extrication from the old Puritan plot and on the continent the prophets rose to rejoice in their freedom from the stench of dead Gods, in England these artists agonized. The familiar term which characterizes them is neither rage nor joy, neither cocksureness nor faith: it is doubt. They could no longer hold to the old verities nor find replacement. An expressive minority who saw through England's mundane concerns and everyday drift, they have left a record and a report on the meaning of the Modern Schism.

Most of them found the Christianity of their own time, whatever its past glories, to be drab, petty, earnest. They saw original minds heading elsewhere; no longer did the third sons of the better families find their vocations in the Church.

The first argument against the old religion was its moral failing. How could people call Jehovah good, if he was a God who consigned people to flame and delighted in seeing his children dash babies against the wall? They found some relief in the decline of hell, as chronicled by Congregationalist R. W. Dale in 1874: 'The doctrine of our forefathers has been silently relegated, with or without very serious consideration, to that province of the intellect which is the house of beliefs which we have not rejected, but which we are willing to forget.'[23]

If these transcendent horrors were slipping, there were plenty of this-worldly indignities and immoralities remaining. George Holyoake, Mr Secularist, and almost the only man who could be regarded as notorious for his atheism, criticized the marriage service of the church because it 'contains things no bride could hear without a blush *if she understood them*'.[24] He italicized the words to let readers know that he was in the know. He spoke for an age which had what has been called a pornutopian underground, providing a mirror-image of its prudery in a big industry of pornography. But not all the poets felt they were ready to move beyond old religious conventions in morality, in this or other realms.

Poets were inclined to leave the questions of morality to the Holyoakes, the Mills, the Eliots. They were busy with faith and doubt. Ruskin speculated: why were Victorians reluctant to probe a neighbour's religious convictions? He answered: we distrust each other and ourselves too much; we will find him and ourselves to be non-believers or half-believers or private believers, finding that the neighbour 'doubts of many things which we ourselves do not believe strongly enough to hear doubted without danger'.[25]

Before him, Carlyle had revealed anything but joyful wisdom and release through doubt. In 1831: once upon a time 'action . . . was easy . . . for the divine worth of human things lay acknowledged'. But in his own day 'doubt storms in . . . through every avenue; inquiries of the deepest, painfullest sort must be engaged with'. In 1836, the age was 'at once destitute of faith and terrified at scepticism'.[26] No wonder that scientists were content with theology that was a simple muddie, that common men took holidays, or that – as Charles Kingsley complained – his contemporaries, fearful of losing the living spirit, 'for that very reason, clinging all the more convulsively – and who can blame them? – to the outward letter of it',[27] expressed themselves through convention in High Churchism or Evangelicalism.

Frederick Robertson could not come to terms with the Modern Schism. 'It is an awful moment when the soul begins to find that the props on which it has blindly rested so long are, many of them, rotten, and begins to suspect them all.'[28] Tennyson is best remembered of the agonizers over doubt. Arthur Hugh Clough probed deeper.

> Eat, drink and die, for we are souls bereaved:
> Of all the creatures under heaven's wide cope
> We are most hopeless, who had once most hope,
> And most beliefless, that had most believed.

These are extreme expressions. Victorian England made its passage out of Christendom without much cocky self-assurance about replacement. It muddled and drifted. People went to church and believed in God. But many made up their minds about reality largely without reference to him. Ruskin thought that 'there never yet was a generation of men (savage or civilized) who . . . so woefully fulfilled the words "having no hope, and without God in the world",[29] as the present civilized European race'.

And yet many men hoped and what they had, they often called God.

IV

Towards Controlled Secularity
Transformed Symbols in America

> Religious change is usually a latent process, carried
> on beneath symbols of non-change. . . . What is
> often called secularization today is the inevitable
> adjustment of the church to dramatic changes in
> the world within which it works . . . The changes
> are obscured by the continuity of symbols.
>
> *J. Milton Yinger*

The fact of the Modern Schism requires little demonstration in the case of Western Europe and Great Britain. What requires illustration on the east side of the Atlantic is the fact that this happened in a decisive and single episode; that in the middle of the nineteenth century something comparable to the Renaissance and the Enlightenment occurred to Western religion.

Great cultural differences appeared in the way significant forces and persons moved, as it were, over a ridge of change to a new arrangement in Catholic France, Protestant Germany, and in England.

Today, when one moves outside the less disciplined and devoted churchly circles in Europe one has little difficulty in knowing what social analysts and churchmen alike have meant when they have spoken of post-Christianity, de-Christianization, or a pluriform secularization. The monuments of Christendom and of Christian culture are everywhere – even in eastern European nations where formal discouragement is often extended to the practice of religion. The historic churches are museums, monuments or shrines. The new ones are ordinarily empty. In many nations, at least nominal establishments of religion survive with state support. But the masses of people stay away, fail to respond, and are unmoved by appeals. People live, act, and think the same way whether or not they think God exists. The intellectual, literary, and artistic communities are ordinarily godless, so much so that one expresses great surprise and fascination when a man of explicit Christian faith turns up in these areas of life.

This is not to say that there are not countless people who are Christian, expressing their faith through personal sacrifices in thousands of naive and sophisticated ways. It is only to say that they do not predominate statistically or in the dynamics of culture.

In the Renaissance men chose to settle down to live in the world, to begin to remove the curtain of transcendence and divine mystery, and to become preoccupied with the here and the now. In the Enlightenment, Western European men extended their sense of dominion over nature and history and introduced a note of defiance of God, of the Church, of historic religion. Between the Renaissance and the Enlightenment, those necessary if artificial constructs of historians, there appeared a brief new age of faith, when concerns of Reformation, Counter-Reformation, and later of Pietism were manifest.

So, too, after the Enlightenment, in the Wesleyan, Methodist, Pietist, Revivalist era a reconstruction of the forms of the church and a new evidence of piety appeared in the North Atlantic nations. Then, in the mid-nineteenth century decades, the breach between Church and culture became wider, never yet to close again, nor to be followed by a new age of faith nor by any major successful attempts at new syntheses.

Minor revivals there have been. The churches did not die. They developed a private culture inside or alongside the larger culture and became an element inside modern pluralism, not a vivifying force for all of Western culture. During these years, through ideas and industry, men expressed a mastery over the environment and a new confidence within it. God and the priests, often shown a decent respect in private and ecclesiastical life, became superfluous to most of those who were concerned with the interpretation of all of life and with the fundamental change in the social and symbolic processes.

THE AMERICAN CONTRAST

Across the Atlantic, the United States in the mid-nineteenth century reveals a contrast so dramatic that at first glance it seems to be a mutation or an exception to the rest of Atlantic culture, so much so that one might question whether indeed the Modern Schism dare be thought of as a single episode. In such a reading, America is then isolated as a victim of retardation or cultural lag in the relentless process of secularization. Does the stylization of this period 'fall apart' at this point? It must to those who operate with a mono-dimensional, mono-directional picture of what secularization is. To them it has to be a single and all-embracing cultural style to which all people in all nations in any epoch must conform. But to those who take a pluralistic and open view of the possibilities of religious change, even inside a single culture, the prospect of seeing the single episode of the Modern Schism remains and deserves examination.

Externally the similarities between Western Europe (especially England) and America are often obvious. The middle years of the nineteenth century begin to suggest the impossibility of sustaining the culture permanently on wholly agrarian and village lines. While the majority of Americans still lived on farms at the end of the period, the permanence and the forth-coming prevalence of urban life had come to be taken largely for granted, by those who resisted it as well as by those who celebrated it.

The coming together of the earlier urban and the later industrial trends was clear by the 1840s. A business civilization was being joined by an industrial culture to displace many elements of the agrarian society. There was an astonishing outbreak of invention. Many of the new products were designed to hasten processes of production, even on the farm but especially for factory programming. Others sped transportation and communication, factors in disseminating religious and secular ideas and movements. Weapons technology developed apace, making possible the assertion of imperial claims. A new sense of mastery over the environment and an awareness that society was informally adopting a fundamentally new social contract were widespread. While these changes will be documented and enlarged upon later, they are cited here as reminders that they were present well before 1870, after which date historians are more likely to agree that the industrial period and the industrial city had become as dominant in the United States as in England.

A THIRD STYLE OF CHANGE

Despite the similar time-table of external change in the United States and Western Europe or England and despite the fact that we can locate a dramatic step-up in the secular movement in the same years, the way this move and step were made in America differs greatly from the ways we have encountered them east of the Atlantic.

During these years the internal or spiritual history of America did take a new turn. The move was made through no ideological assault from without nor through radical formal theological revision from within. There seemed to be less neglect of historic spiritual concerns through adaptation to scientific, industrial, practical life than in England. To put it as pointedly as possible: institutional religion in America not only survived but greatly expanded and progressed. But religious forces accepted a division of labour; they were boxed in. In the new social contract, religion acquiesced in the assignment to address itself to the personal, familial, and leisured sectors of life while the public dimensions – political, social, economic, cultural – were to become autonomous or to pass under the control of other kinds of tutelage. This accepted new contract was a novelty in Western culture, even if it has come to be regarded as normative by many later American Christians, especially the conservatives.

The Modern Schism in America led to division along these lines; an outer, encompassing culture existed independently of an inner, sequestered, largely ecclesiastical religious culture within. It is possible to speak after these years of the privatizing of religion. It happens that the religious leaders have not had to accept complete isolation on their side of the line. They are permitted to do some monitoring, some inspiring, and some legitimatizing of the larger culture, largely through devotional intrusions as opposed to substantive ones. (For example: invocations precede and bene-dictions follow legislative assemblies and public events.) But cus-todians of religious traditions are not ordinarily expected to offer systematic comment on the substance of the legislation or the character of the event. Such attempts are regarded as 'meddling in politics'.

Meanwhile, individual believers (but not clusters or whole

bodies) from the religious communities are allowed to commute between the two entities on each side of the Modern Schism in the United States. The citizen may be formed by a common and social religious vision, but he is to witness or work for it only as an isolated individual *entrepreneur*. The historical background for this settlement will be detailed in the following pages.

Because the American version of secularization, which amounts to the abandonment of some but not all areas of life, represents a controlled and manipulated process, it is a complex one. The secular does not stand out in bold outline against the background of an historic sacral culture. So long as people do not intrude across the lines of the cultures left by the schism, there is little tension or militancy. Ideology is a minor note.

For these reasons, one school of thought, in observing the process, is inclined to suggest that the American version represents a lack of fulfilment, a cultural lag. In this 'just you wait' philosophy of history, secularization means one thing and is to occur on a single predictable line.

Nineteenth-century America, then, simply calls for the historian to be patient as he watches the retarded ones beginning to catch up. A secularist may 'know' this through an imported metaphysic which lets him perceive the meaning and outcome of history. He 'knows' that institutional religion can only dwindle. The historian may have his hunches that such a process is underway, but he cannot be moved by them, since he must be content with understanding what has happened. Secularization on the European ideological model had simply not occurred in the nineteenth century.

Another school of observers, some of them inside American evangelical and catholic churches and others of them devoted to a generalized national religion, hold to an alternative theory. Maybe God in his providence did set aside America for a different purpose. Maybe this 'last, best hope of earth' is also to be a last, best hope for true religion. America, in that instance, may succeed in remaining at least potentially an island, an individual pocket of resistance to a relentless modern trend.

Those who adhere to this school do not differ much from the secular-determinists. They reveal that in their heart of hearts they know that in the outcome of history men and societies will be godless and secular, that mastery of environment and modern styles of thought lead to a non-religious or even anti-religious mode. They see religion to be based upon an historic deposit which must be carefully guarded and insulated, to be expended slowly. Eventually, perhaps, it will disappear from history, but careful custodians can at least retard the process and guard the deposit in a peculiar nation like the United States.

In the face of this mentality the historian is also slow to speak. He does not know enough about inevitable outcomes in history. He may again have his private hunches, but his main goal is to understand what has happened. And what has happened so far, as demonstrated chiefly in the American version of the Modern Schism, is something quite different but not less profound from what happened elsewhere in the West.

A careful study of the documents and traces left by churchmen, societal leaders, common people, and foreign visitors, suggests a third style, a third path towards a kind of secular transformation of culture. When America moved over the hump of change into a new age its people carried many religious elements fused with some new secular ones. Their landscape is somewhat more confused than was the European terrain. Their resolution would have to be described as somehow 'religio-secular' or mixed.

Such an observation cannot serve as a basis for future prophesy: the historian is not sure, either, that this particular resolution is permanent or represents what will be an outcome in history. He must even take the risk that in setting forth this account as a basis of understanding the past and present, it may mislead those who wish to anticipate the future. America may very well be experiencing its upheaval or fault in the twentieth century as the continent did in the nineteenth. The risk of misguiding activists is present, but the student of history has to take it, believing that he can do no more than provide as accurate an accounting of the past as possible.

The American story is so complex because of an intricate process which is repeated in the records of numberless religious leaders and spokesmen in the nineteenth century. They ingeniously controlled the symbols of religion as they related to society and personal life in such a way that radical religious change could occur without a disruption in the continuity of those symbols. Superficially, these remained as they had been, but their substance or that to which they purportedly referred, was often altered.

This process, which will receive ample documentation, does justice to the new this-worldliness of the Americans of the 1870s (compared with the language of other-worldliness of many of their fathers in the 1830s), just as it helps account for the modes of survival of religious institutions and symbols. Because of it, the Modern Schism, which saw a parting between two vital entities, the secular public culture and the private churchly culture, was masked or disguised. Thus there was no demise of religion. On the contrary, a larger percentage of the American people attended and belonged to church in 1876 than in 1776, in 1870 than in 1830 – in any later year of record than in any earlier year. Religion did not disappear; it was relocated. Through its symbols, people were able to undergo epochal shifts and changes without feeling the full force of transition: they could claim to be making the move under the tutelage of traditional leaders using conventional religious symbols.

AN EXPERIMENT WITH TEXTBOOKS

Anyone can make an experiment which will demonstrate the point about the relocation of religion in American culture. Take any two-volume or two-part sourcebook on American history, preferably one which breaks somewhere around Jacksonian times.

Volume one or part one could be used in any course on American religious history. Its documents would be ready for such a purpose. Volume two or part two would be virtually useless. Volume one would include the pious intentions of discoverers, explorers, colonizers, and missionaries who established a home and confronted the natives in the New World. Many of its documents would bear heavy metaphysical and theological interpretations of colonial life. The covenants and compacts of the early communities would be there. The battles over Church and state, whether united or separated; the witch trials; the legal codes and penalties; the charters; the debates over the Sabbath; the reports on the Great Awakenings; the pages from the New England primer; the role of the clergyman; the comments on morality; the theistic and deistic views of Enlightened statesmen and theorists; the preachers' calls for revolution – these are but samples which show how all of life was to be interpreted and changed by religion.

Volume two or part two would differ vastly. (Were it a source-book on religion alone, it would have to be much larger than part one – there is so much more to cover!) Now and then religious elements would be included, but these would usually be in separate and segregated sections on religion. Legal separation of Church and state has occurred by the period covered in volume two, so the formal political story can be told without reference to most institutional religion. Religious pluralism was manifest after the major immigrations, and with the growth of interaction based on improved transportation, commerce, and communication; therefore no single religious tradition can serve any longer for all of society. Yet we know that there were more churches, more clergy, more laymen, more expenditures and efforts on behalf of religion in the later period.

Such an illustrative experiment is not designed to suggest that the old documents of a more unified or organic society indicated the good old days from which later America fell. It does not point to a world which twentieth-century institutionalists would find to their liking, for in that long-ago, church attendance and member-ship was very low. Only about 6 per cent of the American people are believed to have been church members at the time the nation was formed.

Inside the organismic society of the romanticists' recall there were the wayward, the mavericks, the faithless, those who would not or could not 'own the covenants'. Many of the documents of the earlier volume or part of the sourcebook may have been con-trived, artificial, prepared by an unrepresentative and partly phony oligarchy. (Nor is there interest in pointing to the superiority or inferiority of the later period. It is only to suggest that religion had been 'boxed in' in a novel way after the mid-nineteenth century.)

TRANSFORMED SYMBOLS

During the years of the Modern Schism, then, what might be called the secular culture became increasingly autonomous. Its cus-todians more and more kept their own counsel for decision-making. The religious leadership was called upon usually merely to sanction the decisions. Thus they were able to help the society gloss over or obscure the change by invoking traditional religious symbols that remained acceptable to the public.

To say that the change looks subtle in retrospect is not to say that it was not violent or that it was not perceived as being dramatic by those who experienced it. The move from Protestant to pluralist to secular official life; from covenanted to contentious community; from organismic to fractured views of society; from the agrarian-village myth to the urban-industrial reality; from the evangelical to the industrial empire – all these were violent and rather sudden moves in the United States. Little wonder that the common man often welcomed the clergymen who could transform and manipulate the reassuring inherited symbols to help him cushion the shock of change and suggest that some things at least remained continuous. Without such interpreters of symbols it is possible that 'mental anarchy' might have been present in American culture on a larger scale than it was.

In this chapter we shall largely restrict ourselves to two sets of symbolic transformations in the historical events of the nineteenth century. But they are not minor, nor are they arbitrarily chosen. The one set has to do with a culture of enterprise, from business through industry. At the beginning and at the end of the period, ministers would use largely the same vocabulary for interpreting life. In each case, a vivid or an implied transcendent background was dropped behind the counsel given man for life in this world. Concretely, the minister talked about salvation in Jesus Christ, about the gift of heaven and the threat of hell – though hell found less support at the end of the period.

The earlier clergymen focused on salvation *after* this life. With that in mind, men were to do their earthly work in part to prove their calling. If they were poor, they were to be content with their status; if they were affluent, they were obliged to show pity and charity to the poor. And all would be well with the poor by and by; as Marianne Thornton had said for the evangelicals, the real differences of earth last only for a short time before they are evened out in heaven. At the end of the period, a typical Protestant clergyman in the same lineage would focus, without changing his terms, on salvation *in* this life – though, of course, he did not fall entirely silent about eternal rewards and punishments. He simply rendered the temporal fate more vivid than had his predecessors. With that in mind, men were to do their earthly work in part to improve their lot and change their calling. If they were poor, they were to aspire to escape that status for the rewards of middle class or affluent society. If they were already affluent, they were obliged to scorn the poor, whose indolence kept them from the ladder of aspiration. (Charity could still be shown.) If things were to be well with the poor, it must happen now. The Social Gospel liberals who were beginning to come on the scene at the end of the period were equally adept at transforming symbols; 'the Kingdom of God' became an almost exclusively this-worldly symbol. Most of the terms dealing with the drama of salvation were translated to the task of rescuing the suffering and the exploited as they now were; if things were to be well, it must happen now.

The other major transformation of symbols has to do with those representatives of the religious institutions who stood somehow in the theocratic lineage. Early in the period, even though Church and state had just been legally separated, they still saw them closely related under God. They recalled the organic society advocated by men like John Cotton, and chose to supplant the old one, based on coercion. In this way, separation of Church and state would partially overcome both theologically and practically in an exclusively Protestant empire.

In the later period the same symbols were evoked from the Bible and Christian history, but with countless non-Protestants now on the scene there was more fear of seeing a close confluence between Church and state interests. As Lincoln reminded the new nationalists on both sides in the Civil War, they were no longer ready to see themselves under God, submissive to his mysterious purposes. Now each side (and the nation as a whole, as early as in the Mexican War) was beginning to substitute its mission, its manifest destiny, its mystique for God – to let it be over God, as it were; to *be* God.

ILLUSTRATIONS FROM FAMILY HISTORIES

One can see the change in the use of symbols in the careers of two of the best known clergymen in the nineteenth century. The father, Lyman Beecher, was the evangelical imperialist without equal. Mr Protestant of the first half-century, he had weathered the changes that separation of Church and state had meant in Connecticut around 1818. Immediately he set out to build a new Christian empire. He warned against Roman Catholicism and infidelity as threats to the new voluntary empire. Nothing, not even duelling, escaped his reformist gaze. He was expert at the techniques of revivalism and argument or persuasion. His world was that of Litchfield, Connecticut – village America. His later career in Boston and Cincinnati revealed that that empire was slipping away.

His son, Henry Ward Beecher, as prominent as any clergyman and at least as well-known in the larger culture, retained most of his father's vocabulary. His sermons have no less frequent references to eternal rewards, the language of the covenant, of Christ's death and man's sin, than his father's. But they relate to new meanings for new kinds of Americans. They were spoken by a man who largely served to baptize and endorse the new self-existent secular culture, to throw a Christian glow upon whatever he personally liked in the unfolding environment of Gilded Age America. God is casually invoked in support of Beecher's political views concerning national destiny – but the old terror of distance about God's plan has disappeared. He could be an endorser or huckster of commercial products. Nowhere is the change of meaning without change of symbols more clear than in the work ethic.

To the older Beecher's generation, it was clear that men should put in a good day's work. But society was determined, its forms were quite static. The poor should be content with their assigned status, finding meaning in it without self-centred aspiration or jealousy, without dangerous or avaricious attempts to transcend their class or fate. To the son's generation, poverty was always a vice. Social classes were more fluid. One must aspire, not to prove one's salvation but to become rich.

In the later business-industrial culture, all men were potentially to be members of the middle class or the class of aristocratic rich, and those who remained poor – while they needed and should be shown the charity that they did not deserve – *did* deserve their condition and their status, because of their laziness. It was true that there could be occasional leakage in the system. A man might be poor because he was born crippled, for instance. But such individual cases could be shown charity without disrupting the system.

The shift from the former view to the latter was swift but subtle; the words remained virtually the same, but their context and purpose or appeal differed. Did this change occur because men had a new revelation or had convoked a council or commissioned research to consider formal theological change? Not at all. The younger, later Beecher's generation saw the direction society was inevitably taking, endorsed it intuitively, giving it a Christian christening in transit.

One could study similar shifts not only in the careers of celebrity clerics like the Beechers, but also among lay leaders or revivalists. In the earlier decades of the century men like Arthur and Lewis Tappan or John Wanamaker, merchant-élitists taken up with evangelicalism, wanted to impose Protestant moral codes on their employees. These impositions may have been resented by many, but they were at least regarded as genuine and sincere expressions because those who dispensed them kept the code themselves. They were in the front row at revivals; they sang the evangelists' hymns; they made sacrifices and inconvenienced themselves for the humanitarian programmes of the Church; they taught Sunday School; they tried to put into effect the disciplines of self-restraint in their own businesses. Not that they or their code were always admirable; but there was a perceived connection between the late Puritan religious symbols and their whole way of life.

Their heirs in the industrialist-élitist culture four or five decades later were perceived in a much different light. They, too, supported and paid for religious causes. Men like Daniel Drew, Cyrus McCormick, Cornelius Vanderbilt, James Duke, John D. Rockefeller, and others left behind citadels of Christian learning. Others tolerated Social Gospel clerics; J. Pierpont Morgan was noted for that approach to charity. With the single exception of Andrew Carnegie, who had some well-developed, self-invented views about religion, almost all of the great industrial barons were seen to be reasonably ardent churchmen. But their contemporaries judged them more harshly. They subsidized a code, but did not try to live up to it. They were in no way inconvenienced by their religious commitment; it had little effect on their ethics and even their much appreciated charities were often seen to be the result of gentleman-bountiful conscience pangs or attempts to get rid of surplus. The public judgment may have been harsh in individual instances, but it suggests the insight people had into the character of transformed symbols in the realm of philanthropy. The change came within the generation of the Modern Schism, with its compartmentalization of religious and secular spheres and the ingenious commutation of symbols that went on as a result.

The case is a bit less obvious with a third set of public spokesmen, the revivalists. Early and late in the century the evangelists used otherworldly language; they still do. Because it is the business of the revivalist to proffer eternal salvation, there is more continuity in the explicit and intended references to the life to come, redemption, rescue from the world, and world-denial. So the sermons from the age of Charles Grandison Finney in the 1820s bear at least superficial resemblances to those of Dwight L. Moody and even the later, less noble revivalists at the end of the century and the beginning of the new.

The difference appears in the context, in what the business of revivalism offers the audiences. In the earlier stage, the revivalist is the small-town builder of the Christian covenanted community, a poor vagrant whose dedication and sacrifice is obvious. He speaks to the really poor who have little hope in the world and he offers the hope of heaven. The century-long growth of the middle class found the urban revivalist using on a large scale the same symbols, but his audiences have become middle class aspirants who hear the virtues of their striving extolled, the results of their industry endorsed, their prejudices against others confirmed. Early in the century Marxist critics could have faulted revivalists for offering religion as opium, a narcotic about after-life to dull their revolutionary spirit in this life. Later in the century, the Marxist would have heard quite similar words from an evangelist, but he would more readily have criticized him for a new cause, for supporting bourgeois temporal values.

These three sets of celebrity interpreters could find company in Catholic bishops, popular religious writers, small town preachers, and small-college professors, to name but a few. They were so successful at disguising vast religious change under symbols of non-change that later Americans do not know how to picture their political, social, or cultural processes other than 'under God', without a specific bond between the symbols and later realities. For this reason, the business community and political leaders – whether they find the piety and ethics of old religious traditions convenient or vital – tend to be conservative and to endorse public support of the institutions and their symbols. Latterday theologians and religious leaders, who interpret and in some ways manipulate or control the symbols, are more free in relation to them. 'God is Dead!' is a cry that could come from Protestant seminaries but not from associations of manufacturers or war veterans!

The nineteenth-century events, understood in this view, throw light on twentieth century social analysis. What is often called 'secularization' is not simple secularization; it is a complex of radical religious changes, in which people act and think religiously in ways which differ from those of the past and from those meanings conveyed by the symbols to which they adhere. They may invoke the Bible, the New Testament, Jesus Christ, the Sermon on the Mount, as ultimate truth, but would not think of following Christ's pacifist injunctions about resisting evil and enemies. They are not merely secular; they have experienced a transformation of symbols, have found their own acceptable exegetes and mentors, have 'made things come out right' somehow.

In many instances, but by no means in all, these activities mean the disappearance of a vivid sense of transcendence or of other-worldliness without desertion of symbols relating to them. (The Texas Baptist millionaire is seen by the world to be the most materialistic man alive; by himself and his minister as the most spiritual, because he demands an otherworldly redemptive Gospel with no ministerial meddling in politics or commenting on the ethics of oil depletion allowances.) This world unquestionably became more significant in the City of Man during the years when industrialization gave man his greatest occasion to exert mastery over nature through his invention and science. But this-worldliness was not of such a character that it freed all people from the task of relating day-to-day activities to a divine order of things. A new social contract was being quietly written, but the rhetorical flourishes were inherited from the old. Prophets from any age would have decried Andrew Carnegie's *Gospel of Wealth* as being antithetical to Christianity. But his generation and his peers could not get along without some sort of Gospel – and they even needed the term.

THE ENVIRONMENT FOR THE EVENTS:
EVANGELICAL EMPIRE

The years of the Modern Schism in America were, in their religious aspect, years of the climax of the evangelical experience or the fulfilment of the evangelical empire, the last moment when Protestants numerically and symbolically predominated at the expense of Roman Catholics and all others. A student of nineteenth-century religious change naturally turns neither to pagans, Jews, Orthodox, continental Protestants, or to Roman Catholics – all of whom arrived too late and who were the agents of change more than the beneficiaries of it; he concentrates on the main line Protestant churches.

These old-stock Anglo-American churches (Congregational-Presbyterian-Episcopal in the colonial era; Baptist-Methodist-Disciples in the early national era) were the chief custodians of the religious heritage as Americans entered the middle decades of the nineteenth century. As the other religious groups came, beginning in the 1830s in large numbers, they found it necessary either to insulate themselves against the evangelicals' culture or to adapt to it. Thus the Catholics borrowed many elements of the work ethic. The attachment to the new American nationalism on the part of these 'hyphenated-Americans' has become proverbial.

This ability to relate to evangelical symbols for enterprise and nationalism was a remarkable achievement on the part of the always frowned upon and sometimes persecuted latecomers. The old-line Protestants did not go out of their way to welcome the foreigners and religious aliens or to try to relate. The fact that the adoption of these modes and symbols occurred is further testimony to their translatability and transformable character. A racist overtone in the missionary work of the evangelicals was applied also to many continental ethnic groups of purportedly inferior stock. Yet these groups made it in America and sometimes excelled in their devotion to Puritan ethics, nineteenth-century style, and religious nationalism.

The evangelical empire had been born out of the First (1730s) and Second (1800s) Great Awakenings, when new rhetorical and organizational genius was fused with a revised theology to encourage revival and the churching of America. Americans came to regard the forms developed in the early decades of the nineteenth century to be normative for American religion. These years of reconstruction after the Enlightenment, which had been the nadir point of American religious response (in the 1780s and 1790s, at the birth of the nation), paralleled the activities of awakened Christians on the Continent and in England. But in America the accent on institutional forms was even more impressive and their development was more urgent, because of the absence of traditions in the new nation.

When Church and state were separated in America – the formal act which begins the charter for the Modern Schism – a new thing occurred in the Christian world. The result: the churches were disestablished, thrown on their own, forced to rely on voluntary support, compelled to devise techniques for competing, surviving, winning converts, and growing. The denomination was one of the prime ingenious forms. The heir of the colonial state churches, it allowed for people to hold their truth in a tolerant spirit. The modern parish, supplanting the geographical parish, was born at this time. It allowed for competition between a variety of churches whose members were neighbours to each other – the old monopoly idea of territoriality had at last disappeared. The modern missionary movement was born; so was the new style in religious education, with its focus on the Sunday School. This child of the earliest years of the Industrial Revolution, born to advance literacy and to promote religion at a time when traditions were threatened, was the training ground for the evangelical empire.

Denomination, parish, missionary movement, benevolent societies, Sunday School, revivalism – all these are what is meant by the term 'new forms' for the age of industrialism and political democracy, for conquest of the frontier and confrontation of the cities. They were all the results of genius-filled intuitive adaptation to the demands of early modernity. Ironically, though they have been regarded as normative and perfectly accommodated to the whole modern age, they were formed just before the Modern Schism. They have survived it, even though the schism has called into question the whole rationale for these durable if partly dysfunctional forms. Reformers and prophets in the later church could try to revise or replace the forms; the meaning-system on which they were based was assaulted in the secular, ecumenical, dialogical age. No matter: they live on.

The evangelical empire in America was not, of course, a wholly united entity. While its members could close ranks against infidels or socialists or Catholics, they fought among each other. Sect fought sect. Revivalist competed with revivalist. Yet to all non-evangelicals, what they held in common in defence of their empire was more obvious and more important than what separated them.

Only one issue served to divide them: slavery, and the tension between the states which escalated from sectional rivalry to the war between the North and the South. The Southern states experienced a different time-table for industrial change, adhered to a different kind of agrarian ethic, and retained a distinctive institution, slavery. Many features of the evangelical ethic had to be overlooked or revised for adaptation to the South, but for the purposes of this story, it is possible to concentrate on the common elements in the two parts of the empire. (I must add, however, that the Civil War contributed to the schism in the culture because it divided the custodians of religion and it demanded competing allegiances on one of the key credal points: nationalism.)

LIFE IN THE EVANGELICAL EMPIRE

The story of evangelicalism is exceedingly complex and generalizations are difficult to form or sustain. However, some common features stand out. The evangelical experience stressed a personal response to the call of God and an individual appropriation of the gifts of grace in Jesus Christ. The converted and responding person's heart was warmed. His membership in an inherited confessional community mattered less than did his choice of response to certain symbols. This understanding was to remain important in an age when these symbols were constantly undergoing transformation from their application to one way of life at first to another later.

The earlier evangelicalism – in the mid-eighteenth century Awakenings and even on the frontier in the Second Great Awakening – was by no means so individualistic or privatistic as it was to become during the Modern Schism, when the churches were being assigned a new place in the culture. The earlier revivalists' call had been in the social context of covenant and community: people were to come back to an organic fellowship from which they had wandered. They formed many kinds of social units: camp meetings, protracted meetings, revivals, benevolent societies, classes, congregations. Later the stress came on the solitary individual's rejection of and rescue from the world, and his 'getting religion', as the distinctive American usage has it. Significantly, he would speak less certainly of owning the covenant or being a member of the body of Christ than as having chosen Jesus as his personal saviour. The movement from the plural to the singular was an adaptation to a time when covenanted community was being over-run by pluralism and competition on one hand and, on the other, when a work-ethic seemed to demand a rugged sense of autonomous individualism.

The American Protestantism which formed one party in the schism differed significantly theologically from the kinds of Calvinism which had dominated earlier. Of course, there were sectarian, partisan, and personal variations – it would be dangerous to think of a single encompassing movement. But throughout the late colonial and early national period the revivalists had to stress more and more the availability of a dependable God. If ever John Calvin's capricious despot had been preached about and offered on American shores, he could no longer hold the monopoly when evangelists called people to make their own decisions, assert their own will – even if when all was said and done they gave credit to the grace of God. The remote, transcendent, inscrutable deity gave way increasingly to a God who was less concerned with fore-dooming or predestining man. The God of nineteenth-century evangelicalism still bore stern features, so far as those tempted to immorality or infidelity were concerned. But essentially he was benevolent and, in Jesus Christ, redemptive. He encouraged man's co-operation and response first in conversion and then in the reform of the world and the service of man.

A new and 'higher' view of human nature, partly the heritage of the liberal Arminians who in the nineteenth century became Unitarians, partly of the enlightened founding fathers, and partly of the Wesleyan style Arminianism, came into prominence just in time to be used for the transformation of the environment in the century of enterprise.

Life in the evangelical empire revolved around the revivalist or the clergyman who was assigned a new status and role. A mobile and adaptive figure – much less the 'settled' clergyman than his father in the colonial establishment had been – he embodied aspiration and activism and was a model for his slugabed flock. He had to gather a congregation, persuade people, stimulate conversions, nurture continued response, raise funds. He had to develop 'means' for routinizing conversion and nurture so that it would be increasingly difficult for people not to become a part of the new covenant.

The clergyman had to aid in the spreading of the contagion on which his movement depended; he had to inspire reform and benevolent activities. His work eroded the old establishment but in his success he became part of a new establishment which was malleable and constantly undergoing dynamic change but was still an establishment – as outsiders among the non-evangelical immigrants soon learned.

For this reason, the evangelical leader, though he may have been a prophet or a pioneer, soon tended to become and to remain conservative. The results of the American Revolution and, later, the American version of the Industrial Revolution, were accepted as being normative for human history. Both favoured his style of life, his churchmanship, his Gospel. Almost every feature of the new social contract that soon became part of the common consensus he could endorse as being part of the eternal plan of God. Nowhere was this more obvious than in separation of Church and state. The majority in the churches had resisted separation in the late eighteenth and early nineteenth century; God had ordained something like theocracy. When disestablishment came, many of them provided theological rationales and fervently argued that that was what God had always had in mind and, in any case, was best for the churches.

In sum: the evangelical clergyman was well-poised to serve as the interpreter of transformed symbols and the one who could act to disguise radical change, to reassure his flock and his culture. It would be bizarre to make the imperial claim that he was alone in this. The United States President has always had something of this sacerdotal role. Leaders of the business community and the military work in this way to unite and lead people and to effect their purposes. The clergy hold centre stage only in our story, which is keeping its eye on the religious sub-culture at the time when the whole culture underwent change. The clergyman could not have adopted this role had he cherished the prophetic stance.

He had to be essentially respected as a conservative, one with an investment in the *status quo*. Of course, he was free to judge individual infidels, villains, or backsliders. He could attack personal vices. But he broke the implicit pact with his community if he called for a new social contract, worked for essential reform of the whole society, or criticized the consensus of national values in an age of enterprise.

When we encounter the leaders of the evangelical movement in America in the Jacksonian era we find them to be aggressive, buoyant, self-confident. Many of them were physically uncomfortable – they rode the circuit in the worst of weather – and all but the urban *élites* had fiscal insecurity; they were notoriously underpaid. But complaints about these circumstances are few compared to those about the faithlessness of church people. The only big clouds on their scene were caused by Romanism, infidelity, the rise of cities, and – for Northerners – slavery. They had begun to taste success and could see more in the offing. The churches were visibly growing and the effects of personal reforms and benevolences were able to be reckoned on all hands. God was working great things through the clergy and their followers. He had given them a technique, a faith, and an environment: they had frontiers. They had models from the good old days of organic community – not from the Middle Ages, as the European romantics had – but from their own colonial experience.

While national population from 1832-1854 was to grow 88%, the numbers in the evangelical clergy grew by 175%. Even in the age of the new machines there was room for talent in the ministry. The men of God worked together until about 1837 in a united front of Anglo-American societies for missions, benevolences, publishing, and reform. Perhaps the millennium lay around the corner for Protestant Anglo-Americans! For all the ignorance and prejudice to which many of them were given; for all the meanness of their circumstances; for all the uncertainty about their future, the records they leave make us conscious of men with a sense of mission and destiny, men who recognized that their movement was making progress in history. In that they found meaning and a sustaining base for morale.

The variety and pluralism that characterized life in the evangelical empire worked both ways for Christianity when the Modern

Schism was experienced. On one hand, it served to blunt the edge of many of the secularizing instruments that had been effective in Europe. There seemed to be some kind of religion for every kind of man – the churches seemed to fill all the gaps with their options. Since the churches were voluntary societies, there was less motivation for anti-clericalism than in Europe, where people had to pay for religions which they could not believe or endure.

The evangelical churches gave some room for intellectuals; almost all higher academic life in America before the civil war remained in the hands of the churches. Much of the publishing came under church auspices, and the churches were only too happy to disseminate the works of writers whose ideals conformed to evangelical norms. The variety and pluralism made it possible for the earliest industrial workers to find some congenial religious option. Thus they could be asked to shun the infidel beguilements of Frances Wright and Robert Dale Owen who worked to organize labour in New York in the 1820s. They did not have to become hardened against neglectful churches in an age when competitive preachers were trying to attract as many as possible. (The coming of Roman Catholic workers in the 1840s meant the end of the effectiveness of the approach in the big cities and contributed to a growing neglect of urban lower classes and labourers on the part of the Protestant churches, which more and more became identified with the more secure classes.)

In the varieties of evangelicalism, early American science was often in the hands of believers whose researches reinforced their creeds. The religion of the empire was well-styled for a heterogeneous middle class. It was clear that America was offering riches for those who cared to aspire and to move into that class where Protestantism was now at home. No metaphysical disease afflicted American philosophy, in part because there was not much American philosophy. Cosmic schemers on the scale of Comte and Saint-Simon were out of place; when Fourierists or Owenites did come to America, they were much opposed and they easily failed. While each community felt itself incomplete without a harmless village atheist, grand scale god-killers on the scale of a Marx or a Feuerbach would have been unthinkable.

There was, however, an 'on the other hand' to the story of variety and pluralism. The corollary, competition, worked to minimize the ability of Americans to unite in a common interpretation of life. Organic views of community were hard to hold in the face of millennial sects like the Millerites, the upper class Unitarians, the lower class Universalists, the abrasive and threatening Mormons, the anti-mission Baptists, and others who chipped away at the edges of the evangelical empire. Viewed from a distance, the evangelical appeal looks united; viewed from the angle of a man who is hearing the competitive pitches of two groups, the differences are vast. In the confusion of appeals, extreme disorder was often a result. Joseph Smith, founder of the Mormons, claimed that he began his new religious quest out of dissatisfaction after he had been worn out by all the proselytizing revivalists. Others robbed the individual visions of their redemptive power by noticing only that which they all held in common while rejecting their distinctive features as being irrelevant.

Despite this flaw, the evangelicals were ready to face the turmoil of transition. Their commonwealth and community seemed to be in order. They already had what Americans presumably wanted. They had outlasted the revolutionary pagans like Benjamin Frank lin and Thomas Jefferson and by the 1840s could begin to appropriate them as religious heroes in the same hagiography with other unorthodox men like George Washington – another case of symbolic transformation! Even the change to Jacksonian democracy was not violent. There were churches ready with justification for its new styles. A Christian interpretation of the metaphysically non-committal United States Constitution made it possible for evangelicals to gloss over the fundamentally secular judicial settlement in America. Legal pluralism was not yet the problem it was to become when non-Protestants abounded.

So the evangelicals, in a sense, ran the show. They generally picked and chose wisely in the legislative area. After a few misguided attempts down into Jacksonian times (as in the case of Ezra Stiles Ely) to form Christian parties in politics, most were content to line up with existing parties and policies. Believing that reform would come through concentration on individuals' vices, they worked on laws that had to do with keeping the Sabbath, limiting the liquor traffic, and reforming prostitutes – and not with those which might fundamentally re-organize society. Slavery was defended by virtually all Southern churchmen and at least mildly criticized by most Northern ones. Abolition would have meant fundamental reorganization in the South. Each side evoked the same Bible and the same tradition as ultimate props for opposite sides of that issue.

Optimism and busy-ness prevailed. 'The way to get good was to set about doing good',[1] said a Methodist in 1828. Attempt great things for a Christian civilization, a replacement for the disintegrated and now rejected old Christendom argued Lyman Beecher: 'The integrity of the Union demands exertions to produce in the nation a more homogeneous character, and bind us together with firmer bonds.'[2] His goal was to be denied.

THREATS TO THE EVANGELICAL CUSTODIANS

The American evangelical empire was threatened by the arrival of non-Protestant and sometimes non-Christian immigrants after the 1830s; by the pluralism and conflict of value systems in the cities which expanded greatly by the 1840s; by the scientific and inventive preoccupations of the industrial order; by the impending sectional strife.

Formal secularization, to the degree that it should be spoken of at all in nineteenth-century America, was most visible after this period, when the colleges and universities passed out of church control and Darwinism prevailed in the sciences and was seen as a problem by many in the churches. The rise of secular sociology and anthropology also later served to help explain much that was traditional in religious response.

Those who look for the breakup of the old culture only when these signs were present, in the 1870s, will misunderstand their character, for they have their roots before 1870, *before* urban-industrial society came to fruition, and during the years when it was taking shape.

The passing of the Jeffersonian agrarian order (on which evangelicals had pinned many hopes) was foreseen in the 1840s. The conquest of the frontier, the rise of the cities—these and other changes came in the middle decades of the century and with them came demands for new ideals of production, work, and nationalism. Everything was 'up for grabs' during the mid-century decades, and during that time the evangelical custodians helped the culture make passage over the hump of transition towards the new social contract with which it was to live thereafter.

First, the externals of change at this time. In 1800, at the beginning of the Second Great Awakening, farmers outnumbered urbanites 15 to 1. By the beginning of the 1830s, this had been cut to 10·5 to 1. By mid-century that had been more than halved to 5 to 1. The trend was there for all to see in a society that associated spirituality with rural values.

Up to 1830 more manufactured goods were made in homes than in factories, but after that year smokestacks began to dominate the industrial environment and factories predominated. The railroads came during the 1830s and quickly spread a network of efficient transportation for people and goods across America. The population in 1820 was 9,638,000. In 1860 it was 31,443,000. America did not yet look crowded to the people of the 1860s – the frontier appeared to be limitless. But citizens and especially immigrants had begun to converge on the burgeoning cities.

Between 1815 and the Civil War five million immigrants arrived, many of them destined never to move through farm to city, as the old settlers had done. Labourers were beginning to organize, though the early movement had been thwarted by opposition, by a financial depression in the 1830s, by amateurism and apathy, by mismanagement and miscalculating ideologues. But the fact that before the fall, between 1828 and 1834, sixty-one workers' parties were organized and were appealed to by sixty-eight labour newspapers, gave the public some indication of the potential in a new class of people on hand to be a factor in the economy and social organization.

Manufactured goods quadrupled in value from $500 million to $2 billion in the twenty years before the Civil War, after which time the graphs turned ever more dramatically upward. The first factories concentrated on textile industries, but in the 1840s, industrialism covered other fields. The mercantile cities characteristic of colonial America and the frontier began to be transformed to factory constellations.

The numbers of the poor were growing, and a hard-core class, different from the old peasant classes in agrarian society, became a permanent factor. In 1823, 22,111 New York state residents (out of 1·5 million) were on relief of various sorts; by 1855, while population slightly more than doubled (to 3·4 million), 204,000 were on relief.

NEW PERSONS ON A NEW SCENE

Clearly, a new situation was at hand, one which does not need further statistical documentation here. Everything militated against the fulfilment of the Union's integrity, the realization of a more homogeneous character, and the tightening of the firmer bonds for which the Lyman Beechers and their compatriots called. The new situation produced new persons in need of new rationales and visions. The society was moving from the organismic to the pluralistic: the *élites*, from one run by merchants to one dominated by industrialists; in ecology, the trend was from agrarian to urban; in status, from static vocational sense to high mobility. At a moment of such profound change clusters of people did what they have done at such times before: they showed openness to spiritual change. In a sense, they were shopping for religious justification for courses they knew they had to follow.

Four groups will serve as samples: new labourers, frontier entrepreneurs, the merchant capitalists, and the very rich. All of them were involved in the new arrangement of society that came in the middle of the century.

Labour never made up a hardened proletariat, as continental prophets thought it would. It was difficult for workers to form a hardened resentful class. The potential for making a move to the middle class was never as easy as the Horatio Alger legends pictured it, but it was at least a remote possibility. The typical citizen was a hopeful capitalist, an ambitious enterprising person. The new immigrant labourers, crowded into cities like New York and confined to slum areas, found little outlet for such hopes. But there was enough mobility there, too, that a militant labour force was slow to organize. Some religious groups like Roman Catholicism ministered with some success, minimizing discontent, and offering identity. In any case, memories of the Europe from which labourers had come usually inspired them to bear with their lot in America.

Most of the evangelical clerics spoke of the new labourers in negative terms. They were alien, Catholic, infidel, lazy. The labourers who lived on in their mythology were potentially members of the middle class. Most of the major theorists of religious capitalism had themselves experienced something of the move from agrarian to urban and from lower to middle-class life. They had seen green pastoral America begin to turn to red brick and grey smokestack, and their ideas grew from observing that transition. This was somehow true of Henry Ward Beecher and Lyman Abbott, of Bishop William Lawrence ('godliness is in league with riches') and Russell Conwell, of 'Acres of Diamonds' fame; of Horatio Alger, Daniel Wise, William van Doren, Francis E. Clark, Francis Wayland. None of them any longer saw the need to adhere to static concepts of either horizontal or vertical mobility. Nor did any of them see any reason for radical reformist views about re-organizing society by organizing labour. The worthy aspirant arti-sans that they knew could leap upwards one by one by their own achievements.

The custodians of evangelical culture found reason to worry about the morals of labourers. They were often forced to attend church, to pay pew rents out of meagre earnings, so that they could be in range of words of moral improvement. They could be discharged for immoral conduct like attending dancing classes. Depressions in 1837 and 1857 struck them first, and their circumstances demanded theological explanation. A Fall River labour leader in 1846 spoke for the doctrinal scheme: 'The first lesson a boy is taught on leav-ing the parental roof is to get gain . . . gain . . . wealth . . . for-getting all but self.'[3] The teaching derived from the revised evan-gelical ethic and caused no small stress on the old ideals of poverty or the explanations of its causes – to say nothing of the promise of a better life to come.

Everyone worried about labour, but no one wanted it to organize. *The Christian Advocate and Journal*, sturdy spokesman for Metho-dist values, spoke up against producers' or consumers' co-opera-tives. In 1849 it spoke for the conventional Protestant attitude: 'Quite recently the spirit of pretended anti-aristocracy and monopoly has revived, and men are again attempting to mend the existing state of society.' How? Through the co-operatives – hardly a fundamental upheaval, it would seem. Yet the editors went on in the language of theological escalation: '*The attempt to improve on the divine law is not ridiculous simply; it is absurd and blasphe-mous.* If men cannot live and get along as God ordained, they can get along in no other way.'[4]

Little wonder that when large numbers of factory workers, especially people who had never been Protestants, came on the scene, they turned their back on the old ethic. The old agitators from the 1820s were gone by the late 1840s. A few German 'forty-eighters' worked among German labourers. Now and then a gifted prophet would speak out. The erratic Orestes Brownson, one-time infidel and later Catholic publicist, was one of these. In 1840: 'All over the world this fact stares us in the face, the workingman is poor and depressed, while a large portion of the non-workingmen . . . are wealthy.'[5] But he was also unsuccessful at organization of their discontent. By the time labour was finally able to organize, in the 1870s and 1880s, some in the churches – like Cardinal James Gibbons – were ready with at least sympathetic assent to their efforts.

A second group of people who represented challenge for the old shapers of values were the frontier entrepreneurs. 'Never, I think, has there been such excitement in any country of the world', said Walter Colton, of the discovery of gold in California in 1849. Oil was discovered in Pennsylvania in 1861 – here was more opportunity. But most of all, there were grassy frontiers. 'It is our manifest destiny', wrote John L. O'Sullivan in the New York *Morning News* in 1845, 'to overspread and to possess the whole of the continent which Providence has given us . . .'[6]

The frontier entrepreneurs, prospectors, discoverers, builders, and farmers were in continuity with their fathers at the turn of the century, so far as the problems of isolation, lawlessness, and removal from traditional community were concerned. But they were also beginning to belong to the urban-industrial network, because they brought forth products they mined and grew, not for home-front survival, but to be part of a complex economic process. They needed justification for their ambitions. No longer were they asked to be content with ten acres, a brook, and some trees. Now the rich hills could make them rich. Aspire!

What they were told can be related to the message given to the smaller businessmen, the less than very rich merchant capitalists. They were the antecedents of the giant heads of corporations who were the 'robber barons' of the industrial age. The later industrialist, as head of a huge impersonal organization, was less directly responsible to his client. The merchant still knew he was dealing directly with consumers. The lady who bought at Wanamaker's store in Philadelphia had to be satisfied with his services and convinced of his honesty or it would reflect on his honour. Later, victims could not do so much in creative reaction to a magnate who manipulated stock – though the later industrialist was often allowed to live with an ethic forged for the merchant and businessman.

Many of these merchants had themselves come up from office-boy or shipping-clerk status. They had seen the part religious self-discipline had played in their lives, rich with opportunity as they had been. These men were usually the personnel of the interlocking directorates that supported the benevolent and missionary societies as well as the revivals in Boston, Philadelphia, New York, and the middle-size cities of the pre-Civil War years. None of these men could have lived with the earliest evangelical ethic. It had to be transformed, subtly but surely, by the clergy.

The clergy appealed to such men for their support and catered to their interests in return. Brownson had caustic words for this alliance: 'Our clergy are raised up, educated, fashioned, and sustained by wealthy employers. Not a few of our churches rest on Mammon for their foundation. The basement is a trader's shop.'[7] This Mammon belonged to men in the upper classes who had moved up from the lower ranks and who had seen a transformation of the evangelical ethic at each reassuring stage.

The self-made man became the new ideal in America, in contrast to the old European aristocrat or the earlier American man content with his station in life. His presence suggested how much change had been masked by a continuity of symbols. The successful man kept hearing the minister invoking the old language of heaven and hell, rewards and punishment. But on the temporal side of that transcendent curtain, all was different. The message was not, 'Be contented!' but 'Get ahead!' The poor were not pitied so much as condemned for indolence.

The literature designed for such persons mixed religious and secular appeals in the pattern of a generalized moralism. Thus in 1848 John Frost wrote *The Self-Made Men of America*, and in 1858 Charles Seymour flattered him with imitation: *Self-Made Men*. The phrase, so anti-theological in the older sense, had entered the vocabulary. At the beginning, people were to make themselves within a defined context. Sylvester Judd stressed the point in one of his novels: 'Show them how to rise *in* their calling, not out of it.'[8] But the America of the mid-nineteenth century could put no such lid on rising. Soon, the passages full of uneasiness about changing calling and about the perils during the upward movement gave way to Christian, ceiling-unlimited language. How was one to account for the successful evangelical?

These newly-rich at first seemed to want the benefit of clergy for their passage. They had not inherited blood or land, but they had been successful traders, speculators, and merchants. The Puritan had been told to be suspicious of the rich. The evangelical had been told to be content if he was not rich. The American in the mid-nineteenth century was beginning to be told to get rich. In 1836 the Reverend Thomas P. Hunt in *The Book of Wealth* wrote that 'no man can be obedient to God's will without becoming wealthy'.[9] *The Congregationalist*, forty years later, in rather bizarre metaphor revealed the extent of materialism that resides under the veneer of religiosity in subsequent American religion: 'There is no sleeping partner in any business who can begin to compare with the Almighty.'[10]

The few godless rich created special problems for clerical interpreters. The first of these, Stephen Girard, who died on December 26, 1831, was a harbinger of future troubles. His will as 'the richest *merchant* in the world' turned his wealth over to a school for 'poor white orphan boys' (acceptable); but Girard would allow no minister of religion on the Girard College premises (unacceptable). The New York *Evangelist* observed: 'Voltaire could not have showed his malignity to the gospel, more plainly than Mons. G. has done . . . It is an insult to christianity.'[11] It was also a reminder that the aspiration motif of the evangelical ethic could be stimulated without the aid or solace of a Protestant preacher. Was theology or piety, then, irrelevant?

The Girard case did not deter the established clergy from their race to endorse great wealth. Many were nervous about the means the second rich man, John Jacob Astor, had used to acquire riches. But when he died in 1848 six clergymen were on hand to help bury him. Among them was Jonathan Mayhew Wainwright, who spoke for his age when he contended that unequal distribution of wealth was not only 'an unalterable consequence of the nature of man, and the state of being in which he is placed, but also the only system by which his happiness and improvement can be promoted in this state of being'. Wainwright went further, warning social reformers that any tampering with property rights, for example through unequal taxation, any feeling that 'men are imperilled and harassed in their efforts to obtain it'[12] would interfere 'with the progress of knowledge, virtue, and happiness'.

Astor would not need to spin in his grave over such words, but Wainwright's New England ancestors would have had occasion to, for the old Puritan economy had implied covenant and planning. No longer. When the merchant economy turned to an industrial one, the rationale was already prepared for industrialists. Andrew Carnegie had to do little translating of symbols to write his book which would have looked pagan to evangelicals a half-century earlier: *The Gospel of Wealth*. The rationales for merchants and their employees hardly touched industrial workers, unorganized and hopeless as they were, when they began to come in significant numbers after the New England textile industry developed in the 1840s. Even though the churches were more successful at staving off repudiation by other classes than were their European counterparts, the American evangelical denominations increasingly became identified with the middle class, for whom they forged an ethic that was misused by rich exploiters and unusable by the urban poor.

A COMMON RELIGION

The evangelicals were themselves divided, and so were the other religious forces. Spiritual anarchy threatened as the old empire found its monopoly challenged. Those who tried to hold together such a precarious social fabric saw the need to try to homogenize the disparate elements. A very informal kind of secular religion was called for. A latter-day Jeffersonian, Daniel D. Barnard, gave classic expression to the need and the reality as he spoke for 'a national religion, as well as a national government'. 'Our only safety consists in having a popular religious sense to fall back upon.' The people, he found, were already bound by a 'common sense of religious obligation'.[13] A lay religion, a radically altered religious construct, devised right under the noses of the clergy and with their unwitting help, was well on its way to formulation. Its growing presence was another contribution to the Modern Schism and the displacement of vestigial Christendom in America.

THE PERCEPTION OF CHANGE

In England the poets and literary figures agonized about doubt when the nation was still church-going and superficially very religious. In America a flowering of writers served as a similar Greek chorus. They saw through the surface continuities in American religion and society, exposed them, and celebrated the new common religion which Barnard called for and which they wanted to help ritualize and celebrate. Minority reporters in their own time, it is to them and to no evangelical clerics that the nation has later turned for a reliable analysis of what was really going on at mid-century.

They represented the first post-Christian generation of American writers, men and women who were formed by and who recalled the older religious culture but who also saw a new one coming to life. Thoreau's *A Week on the Concord and Merrimac Rivers* manifested the new pantheism in 1849. A year later, Nathaniel Hawthorne's *Scarlet Letter* revealed how far thoughtful Americans had come from the days when devotion to colonial Puritan virtues could be taken for granted. In 1851 Herman Melville took biblical and Christian mythical materials out of the colonial past and fused them into a new myth in *Moby Dick*. Thoreau's *Walden* appeared in 1854; here was a man standing at an *axis mundi* where he could repudiate Christian historical development, the churches, the business society, urbanization, and industrialization all at once in the name of a new ethic and a new spirituality. In 1855 Walt Whitman's *Leaves of Grass* revealed the extent of the new paganism. It is questionable whether any other seven years of national history provide Americans with so many comparable definitions of the American experience in fresh terms.

These intellectuals found new forums. The colleges were still under evangelical control. But the lyceum became the rage, as people attended lectures which began to supplant what sermons had once given many of them. They congregated at places like Brook Farm or in one or another of the experimental communities. Publishing houses like Harper Brothers invaded the homes with literature to compete with that of the colporteurs of the evangelical piety. While the new transcendentalists' metaphysics appear today as dated as the world view of the evangelicals, their moral judgments provide a mirror-image of the evangelicals' ethical positions. And their reporters' instincts fused with artists' visions compel attention even now. To them we shall turn regularly for a parallel reading. They demonstrate that awareness of the meaning of change was widespread forty years before the industrial order came to fulfilment; they foresaw the religious consequences.

Ralph Waldo Emerson saw the issues in cosmic historical terms of faith and non-faith. While the evangelicals assured themselves that everything would be basically all right (except for residual vices) if everyone turned to them, Emerson discussed a spiritual malaise. Every age, like every human body, argued Emerson, has its own distemper. 'Our forefathers walked in the world and went to their graves, tormented with the fear of Sin, and the Terror of the Day of Judgment.' So much for life behind the cosmic screen of transcendence. 'These terrors have lost their force, and our torment is unbelief, the uncertainty as to what we ought to do.'[14] The schism was here, but so far only the prophets knew it; the public groped its way.

To the preachers unbelief was nothing but the refusal to respond to their appeals to come to Jesus. Emerson described unbelief as the directionless spiritual life of the gain and grasp culture endorsed by the preachers – in other words, their belief was his unbelief; their revised ethic was to his mind the final immorality. Their fathers might well have agreed with his analysis, though certainly not with his therapy.

These writers sensed not only, as Emerson did, that the industrial revolution would tear up organismic views of community and religious values associated with them. It would also destroy the organic view of undisturbed nature. No one saw this better than Hawthorne who, in 1844, recorded in his journal his thoughts occasioned by a locomotive interrupting pastoral beauty and calm. All was 'unquietness'[15] from then on. Two millenniums of pastoral imagery from the Bible had nurtured the spirituality of the West. These men knew what has turned out to be widely recognized: that the development of an urban spirituality – the kind of thing Walt Whitman sought – would be a difficult task, one that remains unresolved in American culture and the churches.

'Technology' was a new term, coined in 1829 by Jacob Bigelow at Harvard. But within twenty years Boston-based writers were busying themselves measuring the psychic damage of technology. They united in their prediction that for most Americans, the attributes once associated with God would now be tendered to the machine, and the energies once absorbed by the quest for God would now be directed to the conquest of nature and economic gain. Some of them were breathless. One queried: 'Are not our inventors absolutely ushering in the very dawn of the millennium?'[16] But Henry Adams, in 1905, reflecting on the world of 1844, knew the price of newness and spoke of another dimension of the Modern Schism: 'The old universe was thrown into the ash-heap and a new one created.'[17]

Most of the writers were ambivalent. They cheered technology and industry as often as they repudiated the city, hoping (with many evangelicals, by the way) that the nation could have factories without cities. William Gregg argued, 'A cotton factory should not be located in a city',[18] because with its pluralism and its beguilements crowds would fall into every evil. In 1835 manufacturers had been polled. They agreed that they wished to avoid the cities, not yet aware of the urban magnetism of their new factories. Visitor Robert Dale Owen joined the ambivalent ones: 'I see that the immense modern powers of production *might be* a blessing, and that they *are* a curse.'[19]

The city was seen to be the root of the industrial problem. Boston might pass for the Transcendentalists, though many favoured Brook Farm. Emerson, who somehow came out on both sides of most issues, wanted rural strength for his children and for religious purposes, but he wished for the city's facility and polish – knowing, he said, that he could not have both. 'I always seem to suffer some loss of faith on entering cities. They are great conspiracies.'[20]

Europe, the repudiated Old World, was often identified with the dangers of technology and urbanization. Historian George Bancroft contributed to this mythology of rejection with a final-filter comment: 'Priestcraft did not emigrate . . . to the forest of America . . . Nothing came from Europe but a free people.'[21] Priestcraft, cities, complexity, history, tradition – these were the legacies of Europe. Simplicity, innocence, fresh opportunity, the frontier, village life – these were the promises of America. The evangelicals agreed with their somewhat pagan contemporaries on this syndrome. They were anti-European and anti-priestcraft and they exploited the national nostalgia for simplicity. In these years a simplistic Biblicism developed, one which tended to repudiate most of nineteen centuries of Christian history. The result was a Gospel primitivism which had room in the nineteenth century for little history except that of early Christianity, the Reformation, and America. Nothing else but America mattered, and *it* must be rescued from Catholicism, cities, factories.

If the evangelicals could jettison history from inside the Christian tradition, the intellectuals, claiming little legacy from that particular past, could do so with a vengeance. Emerson divided the nation into 'the party of the Past and the party of the Future.' A character in Hawthorne's *Earth's Holocaust* put it this way: 'Now we shall get rid of the weight of dead men's thoughts.'[23]

At the centre of the party of the past was the remnant of that limiting doctrine of the Fall, which the evangelicals still had to preach in order to stimulate belief in a salvation from sin. 'The whole system of beliefs which came in with the story of the "fall of man",' wrote Oliver Wendell Holmes, was now 'gently fading out of enlightened intelligence'.[24] Some of the religious fought back. Brownson, now a Roman Catholic, criticized the rejectors of the past. He attacked Bancroft for his pantheist optimism. Caleb Sprague Henry in 1855 wrote for the evangelicals that Bancroft's pernicious rigmarole would lead people to accept the present state of the world.

ENTER THE FOREIGN VISITORS

Foreign visitors and native critics alike were most disturbed by the transformation of symbols whereby advocates of the Christian Gospel, long designated to offer solace to the helpless, were now needed to trigger or justify the merchant and industrial economies. Or they would argue that the evangelical empire was being drained of its own resources in order to support uncritically the claims of democracy and of a young and ambitious nation.

The foreign visitors first. Everyone remarked on the all-pervasiveness of religion in the evangelical empire. Harriet Martineau knew that it mattered little what religion a man held to, so long as he was religious. Her observation was largely correct; however much the churches cherished their differences, in the society at large the fact of religious response was more important than the type or quality of participation. Gustave Beaumont said that a man would be 'looked on as a *Brute*'[25] if he did not belong to any religion; this was a shocking contrast to the Europe de Tocqueville knew. De Tocqueville also commented on doctrinal blurriness. 'You will hear morality preached, of dogma not a word. Nothing which can at all shock the neighbour; nothing which can arouse the idea of dissent.'[26] Religion was like the medicine of his forefathers' day: 'If it doesn't do any good, one seems to say, at least it can do no harm.'[27]

The visitors regularly commented on the informal pact the clerics were making with the larger society, the boxed-in role they were accepting. They avoided comment on anything that might tear up the social fabric. Miss Martineau, observing the evangelicals' general silence on slavery, gave the most devastating picture. 'They who uphold a faith which shall remove mountains . . . are the most timid class of society.' Religion, in their hands, was an opium. They were meek administrators, the most backward and timid class in society, self-exiled from the great moral questions of the time. One commentator told her, 'You know the clergy are looked upon by all grown men as a sort of people between men and women.' They dealt with 'weak members of society, women and superstitious men. By such they are called "faithful guardians".'[28]

De Tocqueville was less belligerent, less acid, and more reliable. He agreed about the general self-exile of the clergy but knew that they had at least a negative power. They could kill off political careers of non-believers, since they could exploit public opinion just as the Inquisitors had done. And while he argued that 'every religious doctrine has a political doctrine which, by affinity, is attached to it', he was already speaking of what might be called the layman's religion, the improvised national faith. The clergy were allowed to express themselves on the agreed-upon social consensus, but not to disturb it. Religion was a 'political instrument which powerfully contributes to the maintenance of a democratic republic among Americans'.

The formal organized religion was another matter entirely; De Tocqueville also agreed on the boxed-in character of institutional religion. 'In America religion is a distinct sphere, in which the

priest is sovereign, but out of which he takes care never to go.'
Documenting the compartmentalization that went with the American
version of the Modern Schism, he continued, 'Within its limits he
is master of the mind; beyond them he leaves men to themselves
and surrenders them to the independence and instability that belong
to their nature and their age.'[29]

FREEDOM TO ENDORSE THE STATUS QUO

The writers of the 1840s and the 1850s and the foreign visitors con-
curred on one point: clerical reinforcement and endorsement were
most welcome on the subject of enterprise and material gain. Clerics
were expected to gloss over the rise of attitudes towards wealth and
gain which earlier generations would have regarded as non- or anti-
Christian by supporting the latter-day evangelical ethic of private
wealth.

The German aristocrat, Francis Grund, set the stage. America was
'one gigantic workshop, over the entrance of which there is the
blazing inscription, *No Admission Here, Except on Business*'.[30]
Business and industry demanded religious zeal and clerical sanction.
A Swedish immigrant, Gustaf Unonius, in a record of first impressions, observed that in all the new cities the number of new banks
and new churches gave evidence of 'the greater intensity of both
spiritual and material activity here than in older communities'.[31]

Michel Chevalier set the industrial spirit into context. The
Lowell, Massachusetts, factories revealed 'the rigid spirit of Puri-
tanism . . . carried to its utmost' and called the girls who worked
there 'the nuns of Lowell' who instead of 'working *sacred hearts*,
spin and weave cotton'.[32] But he argued that contemporary churches
abdicated their leadership in order to keep their private preserves
safe. They permitted all kinds of evils to grow. He regretted this,
mourning that 'religion makes no effort to resume the helm and
recover her authority'.[33]

Some of the foreign observers did bring anti-cleric biases; not all
are reliable. But the witness of hundreds of visitors from many
countries and many religious backgrounds is virtually unanimous
on several ideas: generalized religion was important in America at
a time when it was being assaulted in Europe; the churches accepted
a boxed-in role; the clergy, dependent upon the good will of the

people, were careful not to disrupt the *status quo*; they supported
with Biblical sanctions an ethic quite contrary to historic Christian
and evangelical morality. Society for the most part was free to go
its own way, though it welcomed clerical baptism and endorsement
of policies about which it was uneasy.

By the 1870s the new *élites* had begun to free themselves and to
relegate religion to a secondary role or to see it as irrelevant. Social
Darwinism, the ingenious fusion of survival-of-the-fittest ideology
with evangelical aspiration ethics, took on an increasingly autonomous character. Even more than in the 1840s, the clergy were
asked to pronounce invocations and benedictions on policies that
had already been decided upon. Many ministers contented themselves with discussing individual salvation in a time when more and
more areas of life were socially determined.

In 1830 the Reverend Gardiner Spring had warned the poor, 'do
not envy the rich. The poor cottager with all his poverty and rags,
whose daily bread is scarcely earned by the sweat of his brow, but
whose piety spreads a charm around his humble dwelling, you
may well envy; but not the rich worldling.'[34] Sixteen years later not
many would have noticed that the Reverend Mr Wainwright was
saying virtually the opposite at the funeral of Mr Astor.

The public school texts, which preserved the old traditions
longer than did the clergy, still put the poor in their place as late
as Willson's *Second Reader* in 1860: '*We should be very thankful
that our lot is better than theirs* [the urban poor's]; . . . *but we
should not be proud* on account of our better fortune. It is God alone
who has made our lot to differ from the lot of others.'[35]

Reformers came on the scene to suggest that the poor should be
organized, that there should be labour unions, that the basic fabric
of society should be rewoven. Robert Baird, the Presbyterian historian, responded by attributing America's conservative character
to the clergy who, 'during [recent years having] had to resist the
anarchical principles of self-styled reformers, both religious and
philosophical',[36] had won out. The clergy were rewarded with the
support of the successful. They formed the *élites* which supported
the missionary-benevolent societies and took part in the revivals
of Finney in the 1820s and Moody in the 1870s. On that point, at
least, there has always been continuity.

Once again, on the transformation: in 1833 Lewis Tappan, a

follower of the relatively conservative evangelist Finney decried materialism: 'Oh this money, that destroys a man's spirituality; and endangers his soul!'[37] By the 1850s the liberal evangelical, Horace Bushnell, was making things easier: 'It is the duty of every man to be a prosperous man.'[38] Not too long after, Bishop William Lawrence, mentor in the industrial age, could make 'Get rich!' his Gospel.

The evangelicals were divided men; some of the old ethic remained to clash with the new. The same Bushnell who made prosperity the duty of all men could also fall back on the static concept of class: 'Men must "shake that devilish envy" which kept them from satisfaction with their lot or calling.'[39] The more conservative Albert Barnes argued that 'Christ never denounced differences of rank in life' – in other words, he would have been opposed to social reform at the expense of stability. 'He never engaged in the project of the dissatisfied and disorganizing Roman People, in the demands for an agrarian law, nor in the covetous schemes of modern infidelity, to break up all ranks in society' or, and here Barnes tipped his hand, 'to denounce the rich'.[40] Yet the men who argued for stability of class and a static society wanted individuals to be restless and to move up through the ranks.

The most systematic and most influential book on this subject was by Francis Wayland, Brown University President. His *Elements of Moral Science* contended that the absolute right of private property is the right to use something in such a manner as I choose, 'and it imposes upon every one else the obligation to leave me unmolested in the use of it'.[41] The book sold 50,000 copies, due in part no doubt to people who welcomed his message: *'It is necessary that every man be allowed to gain all that he can.'*[42]

The clergy tended to welcome technology as part of God's plan for subduing nature and making individuals rich, but they did fear the cities. The cities were gathering places for reformers and radicals, where people of competing value systems could mingle with new immigrants and disrupt the stability and class situation which supported the evangelical empire. 'Don't be in too great haste to get hold of the cities . . . Kindle *back fires*',[43] was the advice Finney received in 1827 from Theodore Weld, himself a reformer on the topic of slavery.

It would be unfair to picture the clergy only as chameleon-like

endorsers of the inevitable changes in the business ethic and appro-
vers of the new social contracts. They saw themselves as reformers,
too, but they concentrated on individual and personal vices. Reform
of these would not tear up the social fabric. Nor should the ministers
all be pictured as money-grubbing flatterers of the moderately
wealthy. One of the preachers liked to sing the line, 'No foot of
land do I possess'. He commented: 'I had rather sing that song
with a clear conscience than own America.'[44] Fortunately he was
content: there was not much prospect that the backwoods or
frontier preacher would ever be an owner. Karl Griesinger, a
German visitor in 1858, complained that the minister he heard
complained of the 'stinginess and stubbornness of his honourable
audience' who lived in abundance while he lived in want. 'Nine
times out of ten this is the theme of the sermon.'[45] But failure to
stimulate generosity or to get gain did not mean that ministers were
ready to risk their place in society or see their message contradicted
by support of basic social criticism.

Why did the ministers speak in these terms? They must have
believed their Gospel – they announced it with rare unanimity on
economic matters. They found America a good place to live. They
came out of conservative settings and naturally gravitated to the
stable elements in society, where endorsement of each new resolution
of the *status quo* was welcomed. They found Biblical support for
the idea of assent to 'the powers that be', and knew that social
reform would have political implications in relation to these powers.
They found urgent need for the development of a doctrinal basis
for change that would benefit America. Being human, many of them
may have naturally sought the favour of the people on whom they
depended. Most of all, they had a positive horror of any radicals
who might disrupt the social contract. Whether or not they were a
necessity for the new enterprisers it is impossible to say; it is sure
that they were a welcomed luxury.

MANIFEST DESTINY AND NATIONAL MISSION

Socialism, Communism, Liberalism, Nationalism – the years of
the Modern Schism spawned many rivals to Christianity. Most of
them made little progress in America. Nationalism did, not as in
Europe where its creeds were often developed by anti-clericals, and

where it became an overt secular religion, but rather as a peculiar fusion of old religious and new political views. At the time of the Revolution it had been difficult to summon national spirit. Loyalty had been directed more to local entities. By the 1840s the more credal nationalist spirit was directed to the United States and in the 1860s was redirected to the divided Union and the Confederacy.

Nationalism plays this part in the Modern Schism in the West. Each of the North Atlantic nations (not only the giants, but even small nations like Denmark and the Netherlands) devised a sense of ultimate purpose directed to the goals of the autonomous states. This sense was reinforced with ceremony and with some sort of metaphysical sanction or religious symbolism. There were new myths, histories, shrines, gods of battle, foreign devils, calls for ultimate sacrifice, and other features that had been associated with religion in the past. In the United States the clergy, both evangelical and catholic, were called upon to give clerical blessing to all the missions and purposes of the nation, on the assumption that the manifest destiny had always been a part of the plan of God.

The churches had not been unanimous in their support of the Mexican War, which had been a kind of luxury a young nation could afford. Pre-occupying internal issues like North-South relations and the presence of Catholics in the Southwest kept them divided. But by the time of the Civil War the simple nationalist spirit had taken over completely. Southern clergymen were not allowed the luxury of disengagement, creative distance, prophetic criticism, or protest. On the contrary, they were expected to be the main builders of morale, reinforcers of national purpose, and legitimizers of military campaigns; the role of their Northern counterparts was identical.

Nationalism receives its greatest support at times of military engagements, but in America it also developed through the need to sanction the national domestic market and to build up a base for foreign trade and policy. Thus the two realms in which major symbolic transformation occurred, enterprise and manifest destiny, were united as issues.

Under the surface, of course, the nationalism which was receiving clerical baptism was actually a competitor for men's ultimate loyalties. The ministers were, in effect, helping give birth to opposition; but this opposition would become a point of tension only should the clergy be motivated to engage in basic criticism of national mission and purpose. This they have rarely been able or willing to do. Here, again, they were boxed in; they accepted a division of labour. God and the priests became superfluous in the substance of national life. They were welcomed for invocations and benedictions on the approved political contracts.

The ministers were not reluctant supporters in this situation. They were enthusiastic contenders for the most inclusive claims for religious ultimacy for America, not seeing that thereby they were sabotaging their own position and yielding their freedom to bring in a prophetic note. That note passed to men like Abraham Lincoln, who, while he saw an ultimate religious and even mystic note in the preservation of the Union, counselled citizens – as ministers rarely did – to remember that the Almighty had his own purposes and that men should be less ready to claim him on their side than to try to conform their will to his.

The clergy also assisted in developing latter-day racial theories to justify the mission of Anglo-Saxons. This was necessary in order to account for the low life of continental immigrants of cities, to establish a relationship to Negro inferiors (both before and after Emancipation, both in North and South), and most of all, to justify America's economic relations to non-white colonies and to embrace the churches' foreign missionary programmes. The implicit and often even explicit racism which tied divine purpose to the policies of American Anglo-Saxons was a consistent note throughout the nineteenth century, reaching a peak around the time of the Spanish-American War; liberal Social Gospel advocates were as devoted to it as were the most conservative missionary apologists.

The custodians of evangelical culture supported these viewpoints because of some Biblical passages about support of government, because their clienteles believed them, and – so far as one can determine from the patent sincerity of their argument and the consistency and regularity with which it appeared – because they really believed it. Providence had obviously set aside this last, best hope of earth. Patriotism came instinctively to men who believed that and who looked around them at a good land. The ecumenical, international, and transcendent character of Christianity was compromised in the all-embracing nationalism of the autonomous states like America.

At mid-century, just as at the end of the century, the manifest destiny was as much supported by liberal evangelicals as by conservatives and, for that matter, as much by Catholics as by Protestants. The most prominent liberal clergyman of his day was Horace Bushnell of Hartford, Connecticut. In the Civil War he could say with utter confidence: 'We associate God and religion with all that we are fighting for.' In less reserved tones than Lincoln used, he could say: 'Our cause, we love to think, is especially God's and so we are connecting all most sacred impressions with our government itself, weaving in a woof of holy feeling among all the fibres.' Typical rhetoric of the churchman went with war: 'God, God is in it, everywhere . . . every drum-beat is a hymn, the cannon thunder God, the electric silence, darting victory along the wires, is the inaudible greeting of God's favouring work and purpose.'[46]

Archbishop John Hughes knew as well as a thousand other Catholic clerics that suspected immigrant newcomers were not free to escape this religious endorsement of secular nationalism. He willingly accepted his role and dispensed the simplest kind of principle: 'Well, there is but one rule for a Catholic wherever he is, and that is, to do his duty there as citizen.'[47] He was preaching on St Patrick's day just before the Civil War and was outlining a course of action for northerners and southerners to take. As the war went on and ever after, Roman Catholics have been as ready as members of any religious group to tie sacred symbols to the changing national purposes.

De Tocqueville reasoned that Americans were hyper-nationalistic because of the empirical situation: they could see their institutions prospering while those of others failed, 'hence they conceive a high opinion of their superiority, and are not very remote from believing themselves to be a distinct species of mankind'.[48] Churchmen argued that Americans were a distinct species. Bushnell, in *Christian Nurture* in 1847, knew that they were physiologically advanced and would outlive and outlast their inferiors. Some other Christian nations would share the future with America; they 'will inevitably submerge and bury'[49] the less capable forever.

Bushnell's contemporary, Emerson, spoke on both sides of the issue. Sometimes he believed with Hegel or Mazzini that in each epoch one nation incarnated the virtues related to the Absolute

Spirit and chided Americans for not having realized their destiny. Just as often he could counter this by saying: 'Nationality is often silly. Every nation believes that the Divine Providence has a sneaking kindness for it.'[50] The Bushnells were reluctant to qualify their views.

THE SYMBOLIC GLOSS

Concentration on churchly support for the autonomous realms of enterprise and nationhood may serve to complicate defence of the central observation of this book, that in the middle decades of the nineteenth century a schism occurred between the churches and their culture. How can one properly speak of schism in the case of America, where the churches were so eager to endorse the prevailing ethos with religious sanctions?

In the case of enterprise, the churches had to depart from their own historical ideals which had made allowances for failure, had given an understanding of poverty, and provided solace for the poor in order to develop later a Gospel of Wealth when that was what the American system needed. It is not the historians' task to point out whether the earlier or the later ethic and gospel was better, but only that they differed and that the difference was glossed over by people who used the same symbols but directed them to new meanings.

In the case of nationalism, the churches had to depart from their own historical ideals. This meant giving up organic views of Christendom, or of local community, in support of the more artificial construct, the modern nation-state. They had to switch from defence of a kind of theocracy with an established church to a kind of republic with separation of state and Church; they glossed over the difference by employing similar symbols filled with new import.

Enterprise and nationalism would probably have developed without benefit of clergy. The clergy, not wholly content with their boxed-in roles in a secularizing world, commuted to the larger society enough to pronounce benedictions on what was being consolidated as a new social contract, a new *status quo*, whether they were on hand or not. In the process, the substance of their revelation, their tradition, their witness was secondary and eventually appeared to be superfluous. They filled a ceremonial role.

Religion and culture, then, did not go completely separate ways in America. A jumble, a muddle, a 'moraine' remained and remains.

THE NEW RELIGION AND THE NEW SOCIETY

The writers, intellectuals, and foreign visitors saw or had the courage to say what the religious leaders failed to see or declined to say: that the old religious construct was breaking up and that something new had to take its place or was taking its place. Legal secularization had occurred with separation of Church and state a half-century earlier: now the corollary matters of belief, ethos, and mores were being worked out.

Fundamental to all these observers was the sense that historic Christianity had given out. They carried over more of a Protestant vision than they may have known or wanted to, but they fused it with ideas current in the 1840s. 'Forget historical Christianity'[51] was a cry. These were not militant atheists or vicious anti-clericals. Walt Whitman was typical: I am 'neither for nor against institutions'. But the historic transcendental claims of the Church were disappearing, 'And the threat of what is call'd hell is little or nothing to me/ and the lure of what is call'd heaven is little or nothing to me.'[52]

Thoreau also wanted to play a different game as a spokesman for immanence: 'One world at a time.' Asked to make his deathbed peace with God he remarked that he was unaware that he and God had ever quarrelled.[53]

The polemic against the churches was associated with a positive programme. If transcendence was threatened, God could be known immanently. George Ripley countered the evangelicals: 'Let the study of theology commence with the study of human consciousness.'[54] Emerson advocated a religion of humanity and love to replace this 'great, overgrown, dead Christendom of ours'.[55] The future belonged to the moral constitution of man, 'and not at all in a historical Christianity'.[56] The American critics of dying Christendom, then, were not ideological atheists: they were religiously hungry. Ripley complained that 'all is blank, and desolate and lifeless, for to our darkened eye no God is present there. And God, my friends, is necessary to man.'[57] Some turned to Germany and France for philosophy and theology. Others looked to nature. Hawthorne's heroine in *The Scarlet Letter* ends in 'the untamed forest' where the clergyman cannot be at home but where 'her intellect and her heart had their home'. Whitman found religion too important to be entrusted to churches and foresaw its consignment to 'Democracy *en masse*, and to Literature'.

Parker saw nothing in the hireling ministers and ecclesiastical blowbags who had sold out; 'our metropolitan churches, are, in general, as much commercial as the shops.' '*Religion* means attending the most respectable church in the neighbourhood, but without belief in the real God, or actual men.'[58] Science alone held promise.

One can make out a good case against listening too much to these literary figures. Indeed, they represented a tiny minority in their own time. But they have also entered the textbook tradition and are read while the custodians of evangelicalism are not. Later generations must regard them as authentic interpreters of a transformation in American culture. Or: their surrogate religion is at least as dated as the evangelicalism they saw to be disintegrating. It is true; they are better seen as the Greek chorus recording change than as a *Deus ex machina* offering a satisfactory theodicy.

They could return, one might argue, and in the spirit of Julian the Apostate in face of churchly power say, 'Thou hast conquered, O Galilean!' That is, their 'church' died, but the churches live on. Again, true in one sense. What happened was that their spiritual tradition and the private ecclesiastical world began to co-exist – which is the whole point of a schism: not that one entity is killed but that two go their separate ways. A final objection: in the Enlightenment in America, almost a century earlier, Franklin, Thomas Paine, Jefferson, Ethan Allen, and Elihu Palmer were saying at least as devastating things about revealed religion and priestcraft. Here, too, as on the continent and in England, one may agree and then point out that whereas the Enlightenment was responded to and displaced by the religious Second Great Awakening, the Modern Schism has not been overcome nor its distinctive kind of secularity displaced by any later kind of revival. After the 1870s the revivalist always comes somehow as the outsider to rescue people from the worldly city and not as the sole keeper of the covenant, calling people back to community.

Towards Secular Education and Science

After the terms were set at mid-century they were acted upon in the latter decades of the century, in the growth of pluralistic metropolises, the secularization of higher (and, much later, elementary) education, the acceptance of the scientific world view, the development of non-religious philosophy, and countless other realms. Even after the mid-century flowering, Christians have expressed surprise and pride to find a major literary figure working out of specifically Christian symbolic frameworks or commitments. Never again did evangelical literature regain its place.

The intellectual community simply went its own way after the Civil War. Colleges were the last bastions for evangelicalism, but they were often doomed. Beginning in the 1870s the purposes of the schools changed. Ministerial training became at most a minor speciality as universities sequestered religion in religion departments or divinity schools, dropped compulsory chapel, and often omitted formal religious concerns entirely. Boards of trustees, administrations, and faculties were rapidly de-clericalized. The inevitable practical concerns of medicine, science, industry, technology, and business predominated, and men despaired of (or lost interest in) effecting syntheses which would unite the disciplines of learning, especially in a theological matrix.

Not much ideology was involved. British-style everydayishness played a bigger part. The division of labour predominated; education became expensive and had to pass into the hands of the religiously-neutral state; some kinds of research could be carried on only if the clergy could be kept at a distance; private schools became dependent upon commerce and industry, not the churches; foreign university models supplanted the evangelical seminary concept. All this was later; during the years of the Modern Schism, colleges served to disguise the transition and to provide temporary continuity. But every major Christian administrator was nervous and their expressions revealed their knowledge that power was moving in a secular direction. The appointment of Charles Eliot to head Harvard in 1869 symbolizes the actual change.

When President Woolsey had been inaugurated at Yale in 1846 he saw materialism, pantheism, literary despair, sensualism, 'the historic engines battering the walls of fact' – all threatening the minds of the next age. These portended 'some crisis, in which the old shapes of things shall be broken up'[59] and gave every sign that he knew he was in a last-ditch holding operation.

Science was to become the great battle ground. In the Woolsey generation men like Benjamin Silliman helped cushion the shock of change by synthesizing their personal faith with scientific discovery. But after Darwin reached American science, the conflict between religion and science could no longer be suppressed or glossed over. Emerson reported on the Modern Schism in these fields, in most graphic terms: 'The treatises that are written on University reform may be acute or not, but their chief value to the observer is the showing that a cleavage is occurring in the hitherto firm granite of the past and a new era is nearly arrived.'[60] G. S. Hall was later to call 1870 'almost the Anno Domini of educational history' in the United States.[61] The schism was an accomplished fact, and autonomous secular higher education was patent. Elementary education was delayed, in part because men like Horace Mann had devised a broad theology to encompass it; in part, because adults were cautious about experimenting with tender minds; some say, also, that the authors were sons and daughters of New England parsonages and hence were defenders of tradition; and the schools were established churches for America's generalized religion. Even in the twentieth century, at least in areas of cultural homogeneity, the schools preserve a kind of religious aura.

In 1830 the evangelical clergy had regained their place as custodians of the society's spiritual and symbolic lore; after the 1870s they could at best share this role with countless others. During the intervening years they had had to change and adapt their views of covenant and community, enterprise and nationhood. They moved from organismic to pluralistic society; from an organic view of nature to a historic view of environmental mastery; from 'be content with your status' to 'get rich, advance yourselves'; from fused Church and state to separated Church and state. They did all this while invoking the old Biblical texts and credal points and by creating the impression that no great change was occurring. In turn, they were free to save souls, reform individuals, and pronounce the benedictions at public affairs. The churches prospered through the arrangement. But the old dreams of Christendom, of a Christian culture or synthesis, of Protestantdom or the Evangelical Empire – these were to evaporate or be crowded with other, newer, more compelling if less ordered visions. The cleavage in the hitherto firm granite of the past had occurred; the new era 'is nearly arrived'.

V

An Afterword About Afterwards

The main consequences of the Modern Schism had become visible by about 1870. The new nationalism was attracting quasi-religious devotion. The doctrines, if not the effects of Marxist Socialism, were on the scene, full of potency for the subsequent century. The industrial system and ethos had become well-established and the urban world associated with them was rising; these demanded an overall interpretation of life as embracing and compelling as those which derived from earlier Western religion. Numbers of new secular dogmas and countless everyday practices suggested how far the nations in the North Atlantic region were moving beyond Christendom.

If the modern world made up of these components is today being threatened or even broken up, it is valid to re-examine the roots and consequences of the spiritual changes associated with the years of the Modern Schism. Not many years ago a twentieth-century Christian, Denis de Rougemont, wrote of the problems for the man of faith who lives 'in a world where that faith is denied, more or less serenely ignored, or, even worse, where Christianity is accepted and ridiculed under the forms of its traditional deviations, its caricatures'.[1]

Coincidentally, his sentence summarizes the historical courses we have followed in three geographical areas. The denial of faith can be associated with the violent and often doctrinaire assault on the faith originating in mid-nineteenth century Western Europe. In the British experience of the same years are many origins of the practice which makes possible the serene ignoring of the faith. And the quasi-religious passage into a new social contract in the United States helped produce 'deviations and caricatures' of traditional Christianity (in which case, according to de Rougemont, 'some people accept Christianity as a guarantee of middle-class order').

The nineteenth-century men were not mere provincials; there was interaction between their national cultures. No attempt need be made to draw thick lines between the varieties of national religious experience. And the Atlantic nations in the late twentieth century are intellectually and spiritually ecumenical. The lines are even thinner now. A young American collegian will more likely wrestle intellectually with the heritage of god-killers like Marx and Nietzsche than with any attackers of American vintage. Europeans have borrowed much of their industrial and middle-class ethos from the United States and with it have imported some informal doctrines associated with it.

The purpose of this book has not been to isolate three kinds of experience but to see them as elements in a single Western episode, full of fateful consequences for later religion and culture. The historian tells the story; this may leave him at best with the philosophers, the mere interpreters, as Marx spoke of them. Those who set out to change the post-modern world may be impatient with the efforts to ask how the modern experience came about. Such a stance may make some historians feel irrelevant or may lead others to defend their discipline because it is irrelevant – it only aids understanding, not action. But there is a third alternative: history can provide little to help men predict but it may suggest a wider variety of possibilities and choice, based on past experience. Both those who oppose the faith and those who embrace it can clarify the roots of the modern secular order (or disorder) through historical exploration.

Out of all these inquiries it is not necessary that a subordinate philosophy of history emerge or that the inquirer justify himself to the extent that he can turn up materials which 'world changers' can exploit for their own ends. In the spirit of Jacob Burckhardt, we have started out 'from the one point accessible to us, the one eternal centre of all things – man, suffering, striving, doing, as he is and was and ever shall be'.[2] If he is Western man, then the episode we have called the Modern Schism has been a footnote, at least, in his history and its consequences help account for his sufferings, his strivings, his action ever since.

NOTES TO THE TEXT

Publishers' names are included only for the more recent and more accessible sources.

CHAPTER I

1 Jules Michelet, *Histoire de France* (Paris, 1855), Vol. III. (The volume is titled *Renaissance*.)

2 Jacob Burckhardt, *Force and Freedom* (ed. James Hastings Nichols), (New York; Pantheon Books, 1943), p. 80. From *Weltgeschichtliche Betrachtungen*, based on notes from 1868-1871.

3 Lionel S. Thornton, *Revolution and the Modern World* (London: Dacre Press, 1950), p. viii.

4 Burckhardt, *op. cit.*, p. 358.

5 Karl Marx, 'Theses on Feuerbach' (1845), in Reinhold Niebuhr (ed.), *Karl Marx on Religion* (New York: Schocken Books, 1964), p. 72.

CHAPTER II

1 For Napoleon's comment on religion, see Adrien Dansette, *Religious History of Modern France* (trans. John Dingle), (New York: Herder and Herder, 1961), Vol. I, p. 140.

2 See Dansette, *op. cit.*, p. 176.

3 Quoted in Robert C. Binkley, *Realism and Nationalism, 1852-1871* (New York: Harper and Brothers, 1935), p. 57.

4 Ernest Renan, *The Future of Science* (trans. Albert B. Vandam and C. B. Pitman), (London, 1891), p. xix.

5 Quoted in Frank E. Manuel, *The New World of Henri Saint-Simon* (Cambridge, Mass.: Harvard University Press, 1956), p. 350.

6 From the Foreword to Louis Veuillot, *Libres Penseurs* (Paris, 1850) as reproduced in a sourcebook, Béla Menczer (ed.), *Catholic Political Thought, 1789-1848* (Westminster, Md.: Newman Press, 1952), p. 200.

7 François Guizot, *Histoire parlementaire de France* (Paris, 1864), Vol. V, 385.

8 Referred to in Paul T. Fuhrmann, *Extraordinary Christianity: The Life and Thought of Alexander Vinet* (Philadelphia, Pa.: Westminster Press, 1964), p. 71.

9 See Alexander Dru, *The Contribution of German Catholicism* (New York: Hawthorn Books, 1963), p. 62.

10 *Ibid.*, p. 90.

11 In Robert W. Lougee, *Paul de Lagarde, 1827-1891: A Study of Radical Conservatism in Germany* (Cambridge, Mass.: Harvard University Press, 1962), p. 26.

12 *Friedrich Heinrich Jacobi's auserlesener Briefwechsel* (Leipzig, 1827), II, 478.

13 Ernst Troeltsch, *Christian Thought: Its History and Application* (trans. Baron F. von Hügel), (New York: Meridian, 1957), p. 37.

14 Max Stirner, *The Ego and Its Own* (trans. Steven T. Byington), (New York: Benjamin R. Tucker, 1907), p. 162.

15 Wilhelm von Polenz, *Die Grabenhäger* (Berlin, 1898), Vol. I, p. 110.

16   In Thomas Molnar, *The Decline of the Intellectual* (Cleveland, Ohio: Meridian Books, 1961), p. 80.

17   These quotations are from Hegel, *Philosophy of History* and *Philosophy of Right*: see John Bowle, *Politics and Opinion in the Nineteenth Century* (New York: Oxford University Press, 1954), pp. 42, 47-49.

18   In Elie Kedourie, *Nationalism* (London: Hutchinson and Company, 1960), p. 58.

19   Wilhelm Marr, *Vom jüdischen Kriegsschauplatz. Eine Streitschrift* (Berne, 1879), p. 19, quoted in P. G. J. Pulzer, *The Rise of Political Anti-Semitism in Germany and Austria* (New York: John Wiley and Sons, 1964), p. 50.

20   *Ibid.*, p. 55.

21   The title of an article by Paul de Lagarde, *Die Religion der Zukunft*, in *Deutsche Schriften* (Göttingen: Dieterich, 1920) pp. 236-69. The article dates from 1878.

CHAPTER III

1   Leslie Stephen is quoted in F. W. Maitland, *The Life and Letters of Leslie Stephen* (London, 1906), p. 151.

2   See Margaret M. Maison, *The Victorian Vision: Studies in the Religious Novel* (New York: Sheed and Ward, 1961), p. 257; the quotation is from 1888.

3   Frederic Harrison, 'The Positivist Problem' in *Fortnightly Review*, XII, November, 1869), p. 471.

4   Quoted in Walter E. Houghton, *The Victorian Frame of Mind* (New Haven, Conn.: Yale University Press, 1957), p. 79.

5   Arthur Penrhyn Stanley, *The Life and Correspondence of Thomas Arnold, D.D., Head-Master of Rugby* (London, 1904), pp. 514f.

6   T. F. Stooks, in *Parliamentary Papers, 1857-1858*, IX, 87.

7   Robert Vaughan, *The Age of Great Cities: or, Modern Civilization Viewed in Its Relation to Intelligence, Morals, and Religion* (London, 1843), p. 305.

8   Friedrich Engels, *The Condition of the Working Class in England in 1844* (trans. Florence Kelley Wischnewetsky), (London, 1892), p. 125.

9   In K. S. Inglis, *Churches and the Working Classes in Victorian England* (Toronto: University of Toronto Press, 1963), p. 3.

10   *Congregational Year Book*, 1853, p. 85.

11   Henry Thornton, *Family Commentary on the Sermon on the Mount* (London, 1835), p. 510.

12   See Standish Meacham, *Henry Thornton of Clapham 1760-1815* (Cambridge, Mass.: Harvard University Press, 1964), p. 144.

13   Frederick Denison Maurice, *Tracts on Christian Socialism*, No. 1 (London, 1850), pp. 2f.

14   See N. C. Masterman, *John Malcolm Ludlow: The Builder of Christian Socialism* (Cambridge: Cambridge University Press, 1963), pp. 105f.

15   Frederick Denison Maurice, *Christian Socialism* (London, edition of 1893), p. 15.

16   Quoted in Basil Willey, *Nineteenth Century Studies: Coleridge to Matthew Arnold* (London: Chatto and Windus, 1949), p. 242.

17   John Bowring, editor, *Memoirs of Bentham* in *The Works of Jeremy Bentham* (Edinburgh, 1843), X, p. 92.

18 Maitland, *op. cit.*, pp. 144-5.

19 Quoted by Houghton, *op. cit.*, p. 66.

20 Horatio R. F. Brown, *John Addington Symonds: A Biography* (London, 1903), p. 260. (Dated 1867.)

21 Charles Darwin, *The Autobiography of Charles Darwin, 1809-1882* (London: Collins, 1958), pp. 86f. (The first edition, edited by Nora Barlow, dates from 1887.)

22 *Op. cit.*, pp. 92f.

23 Alfred W. W. Dale, *Life of R. W. Dale of Birmingham* (London, 1898), p. 312.

24 Quoted by A. O. J. Cockshut, *The Unbelievers: English Agnostic Thought 1840-1890* (New York: New York University Press, 1966), p. 162.

25 John Ruskin, *Stones of Venice* in *Works*, (ed. E. T. Cook and A. Wedderburn), (London, 1904), XI, 132.

26 Thomas Carlyle, 'Characteristics' (1831) in *Critical and Miscellaneous Essays* in *The Works of Thomas Carlyle* (ed. H. D. Traill), (New York, 1900-01), Vol. III, p. 30, and 'Sir Walter Scott' in *Works*, Vol. IV, p. 49.

27 Charles Kingsley, *Yeast: A Problem* (New York, 1888), p. xviii.

28 Stopford A. Brooke, (ed.), *Life of Frederick W. Robertson* (London, 1868), p. 82.

29 John Ruskin, *Modern Painters* in *Works*, Vol. V, pp. 321-22.

CHAPTER IV

1 'Class Meetings Formed into Tract Societies' in *The Christian Advocate and Journal*, II (1828), p. 81.

2 Lyman Beecher, *Address of the Charitable Society for the Education of Indigent Pious Young Men for the Ministry of the Gospel* (Concord, Mass., 1820), p. 20.

3 *Voice of Industry*, April 3, 1846.

4 Quoted in John R. Commons and others, *History of Labour in the United States* (New York: Macmillan, 1918), Vol. I, p. 571. The quotation dates from 1849.

5 From the *Boston Quarterly Review*, III (July, 1840, 366-395) as reproduced in Edwin C. Rozwenc, ed., *Ideology and Power in the Age of Jackson* (New York: New York University Press, 1964), p. 322.

6 John L. O'Sullivan, New York *Morning News*, Dec. 27, 1845.

7 Rozwenc, *op. cit.*, p. 324.

8 Sylvester Judd, introducing his novel *Richard Edney and the Governor's Family* (Boston, 1850), p. 467.

9 Quoted in Gerald Carson, *The Polite Americans* (New York: William Morrow and Co., 1966), p. 84.

10 *The Congregationalist*, June 21, 1876, p. 196.

11 Sigmund Diamond, *The Reputation of The American Businessman* (Cambridge, Mass.: Harvard University Press, 1955), pp. 6, 9, 16.

12 *Thirty-Four Sermons by the Rev. Jonathan Mayhew Wainwright* (New York, 1856), pp. 173-75.

13 Daniel D. Barnard, *Plea for Social and Popular Repose*, quoted in Arthur Schlesinger, Jr., *The Age of Jackson* (Boston: Little, Brown and Co., 1945), p. 352.

14 Ralph Waldo Emerson, *The Prose Works of Ralph Waldo Emerson* (Boston, 1870), Vol. I, p. 154.

148   *The Modern Schism*

15   This passage from Hawthorne's journal becomes the keynote for Leo
Marx, *The Machine in the Garden* (New York: Oxford University Press,
1964).
16   'Improved Hay-Maker' in *The Scientific American*, II, No. 14 (Mar.
31, 1860), p. 216.
17   Henry Adams, *The Education of Henry Adams: an Autobiography*
(Boston and New York: Houghton Mifflin, 1918), p. 5.
18   In Charles L. Sanford, *The Quest for Paradise: Europe and the
American Moral Imagination* (Urbana, Ill.: University of Illinois Press,
1961), p. 164.
19   Robert Dale Owen, 'Wealth and Misery' in *Popular Tracts* (New
York: 1830), p. 14.
20   *The Correspondence of Thomas Carlyle and Ralph Waldo Emerson
1834-1872* (Boston, 1883), Vol. I, p. 269.
21   George Bancroft, *History of the United States* (Boston, 1827), Vol.
II, pp. 453f.
22   See R. W. B. Lewis, *The American Adam: Innocence Tragedy and
Tradition in the Nineteenth Century* (Chicago: University of Chicago Press,
1955), p. 7.
23   Lewis, *op. cit.*, p. 14.
24   *Ibid.*, p. 37.
25   Gustave Auguste Beaumont, in George Wilson Pierson, *Tocqueville
in America* (Garden City, N.Y.: Doubleday & Co., abridged edition, 1959), p.
46.
26   Tocqueville's essay is reproduced by Pierson, *op. cit.*, p. 99.
27   *Ibid.*, p. 100.
28   Harriet Martineau, *Society in America* (New York, 1837), Vol. II,
pp. 350-362.
29   Alexis de Tocqueville, from excerpts in Dan Herr and Joel Wells
(ed.), *Through Other Eyes* (Westminster, Maryland: Newman Press, 1965),
p. 33.
30   Francis S. Grund, *The Americans in their Moral, Social, and Political
Relations* (London, 1837), Vol. II, p. 5.
31   Gustaf Unonius, *A Pioneer in Northwest America, 1841-1858*. Edited
by Nils W. Olsson. (Minneapolis: University of Minnesota Press, 1950), p. 77.
32   Michel Chevalier, *Society, Manners, and Politics in the United States*
(Boston, 1839), pp. 129, 143.
33   As reproduced by Herr and Wells, *op. cit.*, p. 39.
34   Gardiner Spring, 'Wealth a Fearful Snare to the Soul' in *American
Preacher*, IV (1830), pp. 377-8.
35   Marcius Willson, *The Second Reader of the School and Family
Series* (New York, 1860), p. 115.
36   Robert Baird in Perry Miller, *The Life of the Mind in America* (New
York: Harcourt, Brace and World, 1865), p. 70.
37   Quoted by Charles C. Cole, Jr., *The Social Ideas of the Northern
Evangelists, 1826-1860* (New York: Columbia University Press, 1954), p. 167.
38   Horace Bushnell, *Prosperity Our Duty* (Hartford, Conn., 1847), p. 6.
39   Horace Bushnell, *Sermons for the New Life* (New York, 1858), p. 20.
40   Albert Barnes, *The Rule of Christianity in Regard to Conformity to
the World* (Philadelphia, Pa., 1833), p. 39.
41   Francis Wayland, *The Elements of Moral Science* (New York, 1835),
p. 245.

42 Francis Wayland, *The Elements of Political Economy* (New York, 1837), p. 111.

43 See William G. McLoughlin, *Modern Revivalism* (New York: Ronald Press, 1959), p. 41; from the Finney Papers, March 19, 1827.

44 See Thomas D. Clark, *The Rampaging Frontier* (Bloomington, Indiana: Indiana University Press, 1964), p. 147.

45 Karl Theodor Griesinger, *Lebende Bilder aus Amerika* (Stuttgart, 1858), reprinted in part in Oscar Handlin, *This Was America* (London: Oxford University Press, 1949), p. 261.

46 Horace Bushnell, *Popular Government by Divine Right* (Hartford, Conn., 1864), pp. 15, 12, and 15; quoted in Sidney E. Mead, *The Lively Experiment* (New York: Harper and Row, 1963), pp. 142f.

47 John Hughes, *The Complete Works of the Most Reverend John Hughes* (New York, 1865), Vol. II, p. 157.

48 Alexis de Tocqueville, *Democracy in America* (New York: Alfred A. Knopf, 1945), I, 394.

49 Josiah Strong picked up this passage from *Christian Nurture* by Bushnell (1847) for his *Our Country* (New York, 1885), pp. 175f.

50 Ralph Waldo Emerson, *Journals* in *The Complete Works of Ralph Waldo Emerson* (Boston, 1903), X, p. 195.

51 Lewis, *op. cit.*, p. 23.

52 Walt Whitman's poem, 'As I Lay with My Head in Your Lap Camerado' in *Leaves of Grass* (New York: W. W. Norton, 1968), p. 322.

53 Walter R. Harding, ed., *The Thoreau Centennial* (Albany, N.Y.: State University of New York Press, 1964), pp. 41f.

54 George Ripley, *The Christian Examiner*, XXI, from an article on pp. 225ff.

55 Ralph Waldo Emerson, quoted in A. N. Kaul, *The American Vision: Actual and Ideal Society in Nineteenth-Century Fiction* (New Haven, Conn.: Yale University Press, 1963), p. 176.

56 Ralph Waldo Emerson, quoted in H. B. Van Wesep, *Seven Sages: The Story of American Philosophy* (New York: Longmans, Green & Co., 1960), p. 84.

57 George Ripley in Perry Miller (ed.), *The Transcendentalists: an Anthology* (Cambridge, Mass.: Harvard University Press, 1950), p. 293.

58 Quoted in Daniel Aaron, *Men of Good Hope* (New York: Oxford University Press, pp. 42f.

59 In Ralph Henry Gabriel, *Religion and Learning at Yale* (New Haven, Conn.: Yale University Press, 1958), p. 24.

60 In Walter P. Rogers, *Andrew D. White and the Modern University* (Ithaca: Cornell University Press, 1942), p. 4.

61 G. S. Hall, 'Phi Beta Kappa Oration' in *The Brunonian*, New Series, XXV, (1891), p. 110.

CHAPTER V

1 Denis de Rougemont, *The Christian Opportunity* (New York: Holt, Rinehart and Winston, 1963), p. 10.

2 Jacob Burckhardt, *op. cit.*, pp. 81f.

A BIBLIOGRAPHICAL ESSAY

This essay lists books which extend, amplify, or reinforce the narrative line of the three middle chapters of the book. It is designed chiefly to be of help to readers whose curiosity has been awakened on one or another of the topics which it was necessary to pick up and then drop almost immediately in the course of the text.

The list is long in proportion to the length of the historical essay itself. Several things should be said about this apparent imbalance. First, it is not designed either to impress or depress the reader by its suggestion of the riches still waiting in the libraries or book shops; it is meant only as a service. Next: the essay is integral to the purpose of the book, for it enables the reader to join the author in assessing the dimensions and meaning of the episode we have called The Modern Schism. Third, there is precedent for such proportions in, for example, Peter Gay *The Enlightenment* (132 pages of essay in a 555 page book), to which we shall refer below.

The essay form helps the reader to avoid the boredom of a mere alphabetical blur just as it permits the author the opportunity to provide annotation. The listing is also correlated with the pages of the book's text, as well, for purposes of cross-reference.

The criterion of availability or accessibility has to prevail when 'for further reading' is the intention. For that reason much of the best literature has to be by-passed: untranslated (mainly on Chapter II), periodical (with two or three exceptions), dissertational, microfilm, and archival materials are not included; when possible, books which have also appeared in paperback editions have been cited. The citations, however, are almost always the original editions; this practice makes it possible for readers to locate the works better temporally. If a book first appeared in 1908 and we list a

I wish to acknowledge the assistance of Mr Kent Druyvesteyn in the revision of this essay; he checked all titles to assure accuracy. Furthermore, he traced back the quoted materials in the footnotes and made many appreciated stylistic suggestions. The errors that remain are the results of my frailty. I also wish to thank Mrs Rehova Arthur for typing this portion of the manuscript and for many other endeavours during the preparation of this book.

paperback from 1966, the latter date would be confusing. American publishers are listed when there is a choice, but great numbers of the books are also available in British editions and readers in England will be able to locate these easily through book lists and catalogues or library indices.

For obvious reasons, it has not been possible to extend this essay into the realm of biographical studies or exegeses of the works of particular authors. We have enough respect for readers to assume that they are able to find their way through such materials with little help, and enough respect for their patience not to try it by adding infinitely complex additional lists of titles on people as public as Charles Darwin, Ralph Waldo Emerson, or Karl Marx!

The citations in the main text are all from nineteenth-century literature; this bibliography is restricted to twentieth-century writings. Here, too, the criterion of availability ruled out century-old source materials unless they have been included in new packages, in source or document collections by our contemporaries.

Chapter II

p. 18 Since the main purpose of this essay is to provide books for further reading, it seemed advisable to restrict it to those which are of immediate use in the English-speaking world. This greatly reduces the number of options, for most of the scholarship on nineteenth-century Western Europe appears in French, German, Italian, or other continental languages and little of it has been translated.

For a general introduction to nineteenth-century themes, *The Nineteenth-Century World*, an anthology edited by Guy S. Métraux and François Crouzet, will be useful, particularly because of its bibliographies (New York: New American Library, 1963). Geoffrey Bruun, *Nineteenth-Century European Civilization*, 1815-1914 (New York: Oxford University Press, 1960) is an audacious attempt at synthesizing some principal themes, as is the well-known book by Crane Brinton, *The Shaping of Modern Thought* (Englewood Cliffs, N.J.: Prentice-Hall, 1963); an earlier version is *The Shaping of the Modern Mind* (New York: New American Library, 1953). Its last half deals with the nineteenth century.

A book in the series, 'The Rise of Modern Europe', introduces the main event of the period we are discussing: Robert C. Binkley,

Realism and Nationalism, 1852-1871 (New York: Harper and Brothers, 1935). The theme for this chapter derives from two paragraphs in Binkley, so it is in place to pay the book at least a decent respect.

Several themes are implied throughout this chapter, but never dealt with explicitly. There are regular references to the class structure; Charles Morazé, *The Triumph of the Middle Classes* (Cleveland, Ohio: World Publishing Co., 1967) is 'a study of European values in the nineteenth century' organized around the reality of a new middle class. The author gravely slights religious values. Several international studies on politics, liberalism, freedom, conservatism, and revolution will be helpful for background. John Bowle, *Politics and Opinion in the Nineteenth Century* (New York: Oxford University Press, 1954) is marred by its outline; for some reason he straitjackets thinkers like Marx, Nietzsche, and Durkheim under the category that has to cover the last half of the book, 'the Age of Darwin'. This shortcoming aside, readers will find much of value.

On liberalism, Guido de Ruggiero, *The History of European Liberalism* (London: Oxford University Press, 1927) is dated, but because of its discussion of how liberalism relates to church-state matters and because of its generally excellent organization, it is still worth reading. Benedetto Croce, *History of Europe in the Nineteenth Century* (New York: Harcourt, Brace and World, 1933) saw liberalism as one of the new religions of Europe in this period. A more comprehensive introduction to the whole theme of freedom is Herbert J. Muller, *Freedom in the Modern World* (New York: Harper and Row, 1966).

For conservatism, Ernest L. Woodward's study of the Catholic Church, Metternich, and Guizot, *Three Studies in European Conservatism* (London: Constable & Co., 1929) still merits attention. A final international theme (but one which will also be studied nation by nation in Chapter II) is Revolution of the kind that occurred in 1830, 1848, and 1871. A first library on the subject might include the following books: parts of R. F. Leslie, *The Age of Transformation, 1789-1871* (London: Blandford Press, 1964); Crane Brinton, *The Anatomy of Revolution* (New York: W. W. Norton, 1938), which attempts to stylize European revolutions; D. W. Brogan, *The Price of Revolution* (London: Hamish Hamilton, 1951), with a long chapter on the churches, and Lewis B. Namier, *1848: The Revolution of the Intellectuals* (London: Oxford University Press, 1946) which is short on theory and long on events. There is too much of the hop, skip, and jump in Max Nomad's *Political Heretics: From Plato to Mao Tse-Tung* (Ann Arbor, Michigan: University of Michigan Press, 1963) but it is one of the few books in English which introduces an international cast of revolutionary characters, including Lassalle, Bebel, Liebknecht, Weitling, Dühring, and others mentioned in this chapter.

There are not many general church histories in English (or in other languages either, for that matter) but several can be recommended. Two convenient volumes in 'The Pelican History of the Church' series are (for a backward glance) Gerald R. Cragg, *The Church and the Age of Reason*, 1648-1789 (Baltimore, Maryland: Penguin Books, 1960) and Alec R. Vidler, *The Church in an Age of Revolution* (Baltimore, Maryland: Penguin Books, 1962). James Hastings Nichols, *History of Christianity 1650-1950* (New York: Ronald Press, 1956) is subtitled 'The Secularization of the West' and obviously relates to our theme. It was written as a textbook.

Two volumes in Kenneth Scott Latourette's giant 'Christianity in a Revolutionary Age' covers this time and place: Volume I is *The Nineteenth Century in Europe: Background and the Roman Catholic Phase* (New York: Harper and Brothers, 1958) and Volume II is *The Nineteenth Century in Europe: The Protestant and Eastern Churches* (New York: Harper and Brothers, 1959). These books have extensive, annotated bibliographies and are indispensable. The author's interest in Christian expansion, for which the nineteenth century was 'The Great Century', and his optimism about the future of Christian institutions leads him to minimize the crisis to faith, though he devotes scores of pages to evidence about assaults on the churches.

J. W. C. Wand, *A History of the Modern Church from 1500 to the Present Day* (New York: Thomas Y. Crowell and Co., 1930) is written from the point of view of a distinguished British churchman. Josef L. Altholz, *The Churches in the Nineteenth Century* (Indianapolis, Indiana: Bobbs-Merrill Co., 1967) is a once-over-lightly that will help unfamiliar readers gain a sense of coherent plot. An eccentric but rich study, Vilhelm P. Grønbech, *Religious Currents in the Nineteenth Century* (Lawrence, Kansas: University of Kansas Press, 1964) should trigger off many ideas about the meaning of religion in this period.

The revivals and awakenings of the early decades of the nineteenth century are referred to from time to time in Chapter II. Two books, both marred by a strong Protestant evangelistic bias, present information about churchly renewal: Paulus Scharpff, *History of Evangelism* (Grand Rapids, Michigan: Eerdmans, 1966) and J. Edwin Orr, *The Light of the Nations* (Grand Rapids, Michigan: Eerdmans, 1966).

p. 19 Karl Löwith traces the background to the proclamation of the death of God, along with other themes in 'the revolution in nineteenth-century thought' in *From Hegel to Nietzsche* (New York: Holt, Rinehart and Winston, 1964), an important study of a number of figures who appear in our discussion of utter secularity. Chapter III of Franklin L. Baumer, *Religion and the Rise of Scepticism* (New York: Harcourt, Brace and World, 1960) takes up similar themes in brief fashion; see also Geoffrey Clive, *The Romantic Enlightenment* (New York: Meridian Books, 1960), a sometimes confusing but very original book on some nineteenth-century 'breakdowns'; among these were faith and virtue.

This chapter also makes much of ideology; for a recent discussion of the subject, one with much historical argument, see George Lichtheim, *The Concept of Ideology and Other Essays* (New York: Random House, 1967). In *The Decline of the Intellectual* (Cleveland, Ohio: World Publishing Co., 1961), Thomas S. Molnar keeps his eye more on the twentieth century, but summons up much historical warrant for his conservative review.

Some background on the philosophy of the period can be gained from John Hermann Randall, Jr., *The Career of Philosophy* (New York: Columbia University Press, 1962); Etienne Gilson, and others, *Recent Philosophy: Hegel to the Present* (New York: Random House, 1966) and Émile Bréhier, *The Nineteenth Century: Period of Systems*, 1800-1850 (Chicago: University of Chicago Press, 1968): the third of these is a republication of a standard work from 1932, with updated bibliography. Numerous histories of philosophy are available, of course; these three happen to concentrate on some of our themes.

p. 21 To become familiar with themes of modern Roman Catholic history, a succinct narrative by E. E. Y. Hales, *The*

Catholic Church in the Modern World (Garden City, N.Y.: Image Books, 1960) commends itself. There is still some life left in James MacCaffrey's two volume *History of the Catholic Church in the Nineteenth Century* (St Louis, Mo.: B. Herder Book Co., 1909) but much has happened to the viewpoints of Catholic historians since 1909. A rather florid and passionate account but one well deserving a reading is Henri Daniel-Rops, *The Church in an Age of Revolution, 1789-1870* (New York: E. P. Dutton, 1965), seventh in Daniel-Rops' very personal eight-volume church history.

p. 21 The dimensions of the book did not permit extensive elaboration on the course of the church's life in Italy, but some readers may want to familiarize themselves with activities there. On the history of the papacy, an old Protestant version of the story is in Fredrik K. Nielsen's two-volume *The History of the Papacy in the Nineteenth Century* (London: John Murray, 1906) but of more interest for a crucial episode, E. E. Y. Hales, *Revolution and Papacy, 1769-1846* (London: Eyre and Spottiswoode, 1960) is more focal. The Vatican Council of 1870 is another revealing event; for its story, Edward Cuthbert Butler, *The Vatican Council* (London: Longmans, Green and Co., 1930, two volumes) will serve, along with James J. Hennesey, *The First Council of the Vatican* (New York: Herder and Herder, 1963) which, while it concentrates on American involvement, does discuss the significance of conciliar events. See also S. W. Halperin, *The Separation of Church and State in Italian Thought from Cavour to Mussolini* (Chicago: University of Chicago Press, 1937) for comment on an enduring theme in Italian ecclesiastical affairs.

p. 23 France: for the political and social background consult John B. Wolf, *France: 1815 to the Present* (Englewood, Cliffs N.J.: Prentice-Hall, 1940) on 'The Rise of a Liberal-Democratic Society'; D. W. Brogan, *The French Nation: From Napoleon to Pétain, 1814-1940* (New York: Harper and Brothers, 1957) and Albert L. Guérard, *France: A Modern History* (Ann Arbor, Michigan: University of Michigan Press, 1959) for its section on modern France. The first two of these devote more attention to the Catholic Church and the political and cultural spheres.

On the ecclesiastical history of France, the new standard is Adrien Dansette, *Religious History of Modern France* (New York: Herder and Herder, 1961, two volumes), which provides more information than any other work in English, though all who use it complain of the translation. Another two-volume combination is Charles S. Phillips, *The Church in France 1789-1848: A Study of Revival* (London: A. R. Mowbray and Co., 1929) and *The Church in France, 1848-1897* (New York: Macmillan, 1936), both of which can be commended. William J. S. Simpson, *Religious Thought in France in the Nineteenth Century* (London: Allen and Unwin, 1935) stresses theology and intellectual history, while James Hastings Nichols, *Democracy and the Churches* (Philadelphia, Pa.: Westminster Press, 1951) devotes much attention to continental Roman Catholicism, including that of France, in his book which lauds the Puritan Protestant democratic tradition.

p. 23 While the Enlightenment and the Revolution antedate the period covered by this volume, some understanding of them is essential. Some eighteenth-century Catholic and French themes associated with the matter of this chapter are Robert R. Palmer, *Catholics and Unbelievers in Eighteenth-Century France* (Princeton, N.J.: Princeton University Press, 1939) and Bernard Groethuysen, *The Bourgeois: Catholicism versus Capitalism in Eighteenth-Century France* (New York: Holt, Rinehart and Winston, 1968). Peter Gay's *The Enlightenment: An Interpretation* (New York: Alfred A. Knopf, 1966) is a *tour de force* on the 'rise of modern paganism'. Gay writes in praise of a serene modern rationalism and with obvious distaste for Christianity. His book includes a masterful 132-page bibliographical essay, one which makes it unnecessary to cite many volumes here. But two other books should be mentioned. Paul Hazard, *European Thought in the Eighteenth Century: From Montesquieu to Lessing*: (New Haven, Conn.: Yale University Press, 1961) and Carl L. Becker, *The Heavenly City of the Eighteenth-Century Philosophers* (New Haven, Conn.: Yale University Press, 1932) each stresses the way Enlightenment thought both challenged and paralleled Christianity. As historical essays, these accounts of the eighteenth-century model of an 'alternative to Christendom' helped guide me in preparing this study of the nineteenth century.

p. 25 The literature on reaction is extensive; see the notation to E. L. Woodward in reference to page 152. Béla Menczer in *Catholic Political Thought, 1789-1848* (Westminster, Md.: Newman Press, 1952) presents a number of reactionary texts along with an ultraconservative introduction. That militant reaction persisted through the century is clear from Philip H. Spencer, *Politics of Belief in Nineteenth-Century France—Lacordaire: Michon: Veuillot* (London: Faber and Faber, 1954).

p. 26 While I have restrained myself for the most part from recommending works about specific figures, let me make an exception in the case of Alec R. Vidler, *Prophecy and Papacy: A Study of Lamennais, the Church and the Revolution* (London: SCM Press, 1954) because of the context Vidler provides.

p. 29 Arthur L. Dunham, *The Industrial Revolution in France, 1815-1848* (New York: Exposition Press, 1955) deals with the details of industry in this period.

p. 30 Invaluable for our purpose is Donald G. Charlton, *Secular Religions in France, 1815-1870* (New York: Oxford University Press, 1963) with its extensive biographies. Charlton's own earlier work, *Positivist Thought in France during the Second Empire, 1852-1870* (Oxford: Clarendon Press, 1959) complements this; see also William C. Dampier, *A History of Science and Its Relations with Philosophy and Religion* (New York: Macmillan, 1929). Several comparable literary themes are treated creatively by César Graña, *Bohemian Versus Bourgeois* (New York: Basic Books, 1964); it stresses alienation and the industrial ethos.

p. 34 French nationalism became a kind of secular religion after the period under study; those who would like to read of this development can do so in the first third of Ernst Nolte, *Three Faces of Fascism* (New York: Holt, Rinehart and Winston, 1966), where Nolte comments on Action Français and its ambiguous relations to Catholicism. Chapter One, Part Two summarizes the nationalist roots in our period, with reference to men like Le Play, Renan, Taine, de Maistre, and de Bonald.

p. 34 First books to consult on Germany are; Marshall Dill, *Germany: A Modern History* (Ann Arbor, Michigan: University of Michigan Press, 1961); Koppel S. Pinson, *Modern Germany* (New York: Macmillan, 1954); Veit Valentin, *The German People* (New York: Alfred A. Knopf, 1946) which covers the whole span, but assumes too much, and the lively intellectual history by Hans Kohn, *The Mind of Germany* (New York: Scribner's, 1960), a work which constantly keeps its eye on the rise of nationalism.

We take up German Catholicism immediately; there is an

absence of materials in English. Alexander Dru skims the surface in *The Contribution of German Catholicism* (New York: Hawthorn Books, 1963); what is there is all right, but it serves only as a sample. I note that Dru is embarrassed to mention that only some old essays by Action and Döllinger could serve to expand my one-book English bibliography.

p. 37 Protestantism in Germany fares little better in English. The first work that comes to mind is Andrew L. Drummond, *German Protestantism Since Luther* (London: Epworth Press, 1951); K. D. Macmillan, *Protestantism in Germany* (Princeton, N.J.: Princeton University Press, 1917) betrays the biases of the World War I era. It is much easier to be enthusiastic about Koppel S. Pinson, *Pietism as a Factor in the Rise of German Nationalism* (New York: Columbia University Press, 1934), which is about so much more than Pietism and Nationalism. One journal article also merits notice: Alexander Dru, 'The Reformation of the Nineteenth Century. Christianity in Germany from 1800-1848', *The Dublin Review*, Vol. 226, No. 457, pp. 34-45 (1952). Of some general interest also is Erick Meissner, *Confusion of Faces: The Struggle Between Religion and Secularism in Europe* (London: Faber and Faber, 1946), which covers the time from the Reformation to the second World War.

p. 37 More literature is available on the rise of secular alternatives to Christianity in the eighteenth century. W. H. Bruford's *Germany in the Eighteenth Century: Social Background of the Literary Revival* (Cambridge: Cambridge University Press, 1935) remains important for its inclusive attempt at depicting Germany on the eve of the nineteenth century. Because Allison sketches in the other issues at the time of Lessing, one can recommend here Henry E. Allison, *Lessing and the Enlightenment: His Philosophy of Religion and Its Relation to Eighteenth-Century Thought* (Ann Arbor, Michigan: University of Michigan Press, 1966). The pagan side of the era is treated in Henry C. Hatfield, *Aesthetic Paganism in German Literature* (Cambridge, Mass.: Harvard University Press, 1964), an essay on this-worldliness in Lessing, Goethe, and the premature 'god-killer', Friedrich Hölderlin. Hatfield sees Hölderlin to be deeply devoted to Christ and equally devoted to Greece, to the dying of the old gods, and to a kind of pagan-pantheist hope for the presence of the new gods who could unify life.

Two more books for the period before our own: Klaus Epstein has described *The Genesis of German Conservatism* (Princeton, N.J.: Princeton University Press, 1966), with emphasis both on religion and the French Revolution; the latter topic was also treated by George P. Gooch in *Germany and the French Revolution* (New York: Longmans, Green and Co., 1920).

p. 42 The most frequently visited theme among those approached in detail in this chapter is the history of German Protestant theology in the nineteenth century. Most of the writings are mono-graphic, but a number of synthetic works are available. For many years a favourite has been Hugh Ross Mackintosh, *Types of Modern Theology* (London: James Nisbet and Co., 1937). Two of the present century's esteemed theologians have surveyed the previous one; their selections and emphases are revelatory. The first, Karl Barth, *Protestant Thought: From Rousseau to Ritschl* (New York: Harper and Brothers, 1959) is a barely adequate translation of a larger work in German; a student (Carl E. Braaten) has compiled and edited Paul Tillich, *Perspectives on Nineteenth and Twentieth Century Protestant Theology* (New York: Harper and Row, 1967), based on Tillich's class lecture outlines. Bernard M. G. Reardon, *Liberal Protestantism* (Stanford, California: Stanford University Press, 1968) introduces and presents writings by a number of major German figures, among them Ritschl.

p. 42 On the history of 'the crisis of historical consciousness', see the tendentious Karl R. Popper, *The Open Society and Its Enemies* (London: G. Routledge and Sons, 1945), whose second volume deals with 'The High Tide of Prophecy: Hegel, Marx, and the Aftermath'. R. G. Collingwood covers some of the same material from an idealist point of view in the middle portion of *The Idea of History* (Oxford: Clarendon Press, 1946). A Christian point of view is represented in Alan Richardson, *History Sacred and Profane* (Philadelphia, Pa.: Westminster Press, 1964), some of whose portions are relevant to this subject.

p. 50 'The world that demanded interpretation' is the world of industrial revolution, new working classes, liberal politics, and socialism; a whole library is available on these subjects, and a number of titles in English should be noted. Basic are Theodore S. Hamerow, *Restoration, Revolution, Reaction: Economics and*

Politics in Germany, 1815-1871 (Princeton, N.J.: Princeton University Press, 1958) and Ernest K. Bramsted, *Aristocracy and the Middle-Classes in Germany* (London: P. S. King and Son, 1937). Bramsted deals with 'social types in German literature' and offers many revealing references to religion in the fiction of mid-century Germany.

Two works on the Industrial Revolution by William Otto Henderson are *The Industrial Revolution on the Continent* (London: Frank Cass and Co., 1961) and *The State and the Industrial Revolution in Prussia, 1740-1870* (Liverpool: Liverpool University Press, 1958). A paperback version has given new life to an original treatment by Thorstein Veblen, *Imperial Germany and the Industrial Revolution* (Ann Arbor, Michigan: University of Michigan Press, 1966); the original was published in 1915.

Evelyn Anderson, *Hammer or Anvil: The Story of the German Working-Class Movement* (London: Victor Gollancz, 1945) and W. A. McConagha, *Development of the Labour Movement in Great Britain, France, and Germany* (Chapel Hill, N. C.: University of North Carolina Press, 1942) present significantly different points of view on the transformations of labour beyond the confines of our period.

Leonard Krieger, *The German Idea of Freedom* (Boston: Beacon Press, 1957) and Donald G. Rohr, *The Origins of Social Liberalism in Germany* (Chicago: University of Chicago Press, 1963) are two excellent works on social theory, less slanted than G. D. H. Cole's two volumes of *A History of Socialist Thought* (London: Macmillan and Co., 1953). Volume One, on 'The Forerunners, 1789-1850', concentrates on formal socialism from among all the social and liberal options. A glimpse of labour in action is provided in a fine historical study, P. H. Noyes, *Organization and Revolution* (Princeton, N.J.: Princeton University Press, 1966), a review of working-class associations in 1848 and 1849, at the time of the revolutions. The churches and religion play a minor part, at best. For the later period, see Roger Morgan, *The German Social Democrats and the First International, 1864-1872* (Cambridge: Cambridge University Press, 1965).

I am happy to say that at least one book on the whole range of Protestant involvement in the subject exists: William O. Shanahan, *German Protestants Face the Social Question* (Notre

Dame, Ind.: University of Notre Dame Press, 1954) covers the 'conservative phase', 1815-1871, and is one of the few books I am marking indispensable for this list; the bibliographies are superb.

p. 50 Needless to say, a bibliography on Marx, Marxism, Socialism, or Communism is beyond our scope. In the context of this book Sidney Hook, *From Hegel to Marx: Studies in the Intellectual Development of Karl Marx* (New York: Reynal and Hitchcock, 1936), is of first importance. It traces motifs in Strauss, Bauer, Ruge, Stirner, and Feuerbach among others. Herbert Marcuse, *Reason and Revolution: Hegel and the Rise of Social Theory* (New York: Oxford University Press, 1941) is a revolutionary interpretation of revolution. The temptation to move beyond these titles into Marxism is great, but must be resisted at this point.

p. 54 German nationalism can hardly be discussed dispassionately after the rise of National Socialism, which was in part the consequence of the nineteenth-century evolutions. Jonas Lesser, *Germany: The Symbol and the Deed* (New York: Thomas Yoseloff, 1965) is typical of the attacks, based on German history; Gerhard Ritter, *The German Problem: Basic Questions of German Political Life, Past and Present* (Columbus, Ohio: Ohio State University Press, 1965) is an attempt at apology and self-criticism. Several chapters in Peter R. E. Viereck, *Metapolitics: The Roots of the Nazi Mind* (New York: Capricorn Books, 1961) discuss nineteenth-century German romantic nationalism in its religious dimensions. Viereck revised a work he had completed at the outbreak of the war, in 1941, for this paperback. See also Louis L. Snyder, *German Nationalism: The Tragedy of a People* (Harrisburg, Penn.: Stackpole Co., 1952).

p. 55 Nationalism turned racism focused on anti-Semitism; for this subject see Fritz R. Stern, *The Politics of Cultural Despair* (Berkeley, California: University of California Press, 1961) and Peter G. J. Pulzer, *The Rise of Political Anti-Semitism in Germany and Austria* (New York: John Wiley and Sons, 1964).

Chapter III

p. 59 Several general histories are useful for setting the stage; three 'Age of . . .' books head the list. Asa Briggs called his *The Age of Improvement* (New York: Longmans, Green and Co., 1959). Briggs shows a fine interest in matters other than political and has comment on religion and science in a chapter on Victorianism. Donald F. Macdonald, *The Age of Transition: Britain in the Nineteenth and Twentieth Century* (New York: St Martin's Press, 1967) is less devoted to intellectual and cultural history, stressing as it does industry and economics. Ernest L. Woodward, *The Age of Reform, 1815-1870* (Oxford: Clarendon Press, 1938) is a standard history. Pauline Gregg, *Modern Britain: A Social and Economic History since 1760* (New York: Pegasus, 1967) is a lively, illustrated introductory volume.

Since Queen Victoria ruled for so many of the years of this study, it is profitable to look at a few of the books devoted to the Victorian style. One must remember, however, that there was Victorianism before, after, and independent of the queen!

Here we call first again on Asa Briggs, whose *Victorian Cities* (London: Odham's Press, 1964) and *Victorian People* (London: Odham's Press, 1954 and Penguin Books, 1965) are well worth reading. G. Kitson Clark, *The Making of Victorian England* (Cambridge, Mass.: Harvard University Press, 1962) includes valuable chapters on 'The People' and 'The Religion of the People', but the entire book will throw light on the topics under study here. George M. Young liked to work with the idea of Victorianism, as he did in *Victorian England: Portrait of an Age* (London: Oxford University Press, 1936) and *Early Victorian England, 1830-1865* (London: Oxford University Press, 2nd ed. 1960). A lively collection of 'Human Documents from the Victorian Age' is available in Edgar Royston Pike, *Golden Times* (New York: Frederick A. Praeger, 1967). The reader will get a first-hand grasp of Victorian attitudes on medicine, sex, labour, sanitation, the home, and industrial change from the readings he has collected.

On the religion of the period, two recent books which stress the Anglican experience are very valuable. The first is the first volume of a projected two-volume work, Owen Chadwick, *The Victorian Church* (New York: Oxford University Press, 1966). It deals in detail with a variety of ecclesiastical topics to 1860. More devoted to a thesis is Desmond Bowen, *The Idea of the Victorian Church* (Montreal: McGill University Press, 1968). Bowen concentrates on the years 1833-1889, notes the relative successes of Anglicanism with the expanding British middle classes and asks, in effect, what was so bad about such successes? The clergy, he says, wanted to work through the class to which it had access in order to prevent disruption of all of English social and religious life. An older but still important work is Leonard E. Elliott-Binns, *Religion in the Victorian Era* (London: Lutterworth Press, 1936).

p. 60 British theology, for obvious reasons, has not received as much attention from historians as has German. For the latter half of the century, Leonard E. Elliott-Binns, *English Thought 1860-1900: The Theological Aspect* (New York: Longmans, Green and Co., 1956) is a good starting-point. Clement C. J. Webb, *A Study of Religious Thought in England from 1850* (Oxford: Clarendon Press, 1933) covers a similar period and extends into the twentieth century; so does John K. Mozley, *Some Tendencies in British Theology from the Publication of* Lux Mundi *to the Present* (London: S.P.C.K., 1951). For the earlier period, V. F. Storr, *The Development of English Theology in the Nineteenth Century, 1800-1860* (New York: Longmans, Green and Co., 1913) is one of the few available works and is sadly dated. A. O. J. Cockshut has prepared a sourcebook of documents on *Religious Controversies of the Nineteenth Century* (Lincoln, Nebraska: University of Nebraska Press, 1966). The controversies are all British and go from the time of Wilberforce to Frederick Temple.

p. 64 The Christian accommodations to the era of Enlightenment are best told in Norman Sykes, *Church and State in England in the Eighteenth Century* (Cambridge: Cambridge University Press, 1934), a very substantial book which cast a more favourable light on eighteenth-century Anglicanism than had been seen for over a century. John Herman Randall, Jr., comments on British thought in the latter part of *The Career of Philosophy* (New York: Columbia University Press, 1962) Volume II. For the bearing of Enlightenment on ecclesiastical and theological issues, Gerald R. Cragg, *Reason and Authority in the Eighteenth Century* (Cambridge: Cambridge University Press, 1964) is an important work. See also W. R. Sorley, *A History of English Philosophy* (Cambridge: Cambridge University Press, 1920). Any of a number of standard histories of British philosophy or of the Enlightenment and Deism are available.

p. 66 Historic studies of British Catholicism are not plentiful. M. D. R. Leys, *Catholics in England, 1559-1829* (New York: Sheed and Ward, 1962) leads up to the beginning of our period and will guide a reader to an understanding of the background of acclimatized Catholics in the era after emancipation. Then D. R. Gwynn, *A Hundred Years of Catholic Emancipation, 1829-1929* (New York: Longmans, Green and Co., 1929) takes over; a study of a slightly later time is George A. Beck, ed., *The English Catholics, 1850-1950* (London: Burns and Oates, 1950). Covering the whole span as few others tried to do is E. I. Watkin, *Roman Catholicism in England from the Reformation to 1950* (New York: Oxford University Press, 1957) but David Mathew is among the few in *Catholicism in England 1535-1935* (New York: Longmans, Green and Co., 1936). Far too general for students of England is Mary Peter Carthy, *Catholicism in English-Speaking Lands* (New York: Hawthorn Books, 1964) which in brief span also includes the United States and other nations, but the synoptic view has some values which merely national history often lacks.

p. 67 The best recent scholarly study of Irish Catholicism in this age is Edward R. Norman, *The Catholic Church and Ireland in the Age of Rebellion, 1859-1873* (Ithaca, N.Y.: Cornell University Press, 1965); its bibliography will lead to most of the available published materials on the church in Ireland in the nineteenth century. While on the subject of Great Britain outside England: George Scott-Moncrieff, *The Mirror and the Cross: Scotland and the Catholic Faith* (Baltimore, Md.: Helicon Press, 1961) discusses some of the travails and minor triumphs of the Roman Catholic Church in the land of *Ecclesia Scoticana.*

p. 68 Among the general histories of British Methodism is Rupert E. Davies, *Methodism* (Baltimore, Md.: Penguin Books, 1963) who promises a full length history, in conjunction with Gordon Rupp. For the time after mid-century see Maldwyn L. Edwards, *Methodism and England, 1850-1932* (London: Epworth Press, 1943). An established history is *A New History of Methodism* edited by William J. Townsend, H. B. Workman, and George Eayres, in two volumes (London: Hodder and Stoughton, 1909).

p. 69 Because it antedates our period, it is not necessary for us to become involved in all the issues relating to Methodism and the beginnings of the Industrial Revolution. But some of the literature should be cited, for it helps determine Methodist life in the nineteenth century. Elie Halévy picked up Lecky's theory that the rise of Methodism helped make a French-style Revolution unnecessary, and developed the theme in *England in 1815* (New York: Barnes and Noble, 1961), a reprint of the first volume of his great history (first published in 1912) of the English people in the nineteenth century; about one hundred pages are devoted specifically to religion. Edward P. Thompson, *The Making of the English Working Class* (New York: Pantheon Books, 1964) is a Marxist's study, full of comment – almost all of it negative – about religion and especially about Methodism. See also the chapter on Methodism (III) in Eric J. Hobsbawm, *Labouring Men: Studies in the History of Labour* (New York: Basic Books, 1964).

p. 70 It is not possible for us to give much attention to the free churches and other dissenters in England, but readers with special interest can become acquainted by reading, among others: Horton Davies, *The English Free Churches* (New York: Oxford University Press, 1952); Ernest A. Payne, *The Free Church Tradition in the Life of England* (London: SCM Press, 1944); Albert Peel, *These Hundred Years: A History of the Congregational Union of England and Wales* 1831-1931 (London: Congregational Union of England and Wales, 1931) and Alfred C. Underwood, *A History of the English Baptists* (London: Kingsgate Press, 1947).

p. 70 On the literature about the Industrial Revolution, I have selected only several works which influenced the formation of this part of the book. First among these is Eric J. Hobsbawm, *The Age of Revolution 1789-1848* (Cleveland, Ohio: World Publishing Co., 1962). Hobsbawm gives reasonable attention to religion and ideology, from a Marxian point of view. He covers the period to 1848 in England and on the continent, but his discussion of religion centres on England.

E. Royston Pike also has prepared an anthology of 'Human Documents of the Industrial Revolution in Britain' called *Hard Times* (New York: Frederick A. Praeger, 1966), dealing with factories, children and women's labour, sex, and urban life. An amazing document from the era has recently been republished in highly condensed form, and all students of industrial life should read it: Henry Mayhew, *Selections from London Labour and the London Poor* (London: Oxford University Press, 1965).

Two extensive case-studies of the impact of industrialism on religion are Edward R. Wickham, *Church and People in an Industrial City* (London: Lutterworth Press, 1957) and Ebenezer T.

Davies, *Religion in the Industrial Revolution in South Wales* (Cardiff: University of Wales Press, 1965), but many more such studies will be needed before a profile can be discerned.

p. 72 On the religion of labourers, the best book is Kenneth S. Inglis, *Churches and the Working Classes in Victorian England* (Toronto: University of Toronto Press, 1963). Readers will see that it has influenced the story of this book; its original research leads to many materials which would not otherwise be easily accessible. Inglis follows a denominational pattern. Let me call it indispensable. Of equal interest so far as one of the churches, Methodism, is concerned is the work of Robert F. Wearmouth, among whose writings are *Methodism and the Working-Class Movements of England, 1800-1880* (London: Epworth Press, 1937) and *Methodism and the Struggle of the Working Classes, 1850-1900* (Leicester: Edgar Backus, 1954). In these and other books Wearmouth traces the biographies of men who fashioned the English labour movement and demonstrates the ties of many of them to Methodism; at the same time, the lists make for dull reading.

A historical chapter in David Martin, *A Sociology of English Religion* (New York: Basic Books, 1967) reveals something of the statistical pattern in the appeals of the British churches to labouring men.

George D. H. Cole and Raymond Postgate, *The British People, 1746-1946* (New York: Barnes and Noble, 1961) is crammed with information about the life of labourers in the nineteenth century, but is rather slanted against religion. (Religion gave the authors something to be slanted against, much of the time, it must be added!)

p. 75 Evangelicalism and its social policies: Ernest M. Howse, *Saints in Politics: The 'Clapham Sect' and the Growth of Freedom* (Toronto: University of Toronto Press, 1952) is a fine study; see also Raymond G. Cowherd, *The Politics of English Dissent* (New York: New York University Press, 1956). Sir Reginald Coupland, *The British Anti-Slavery Movement* (London: T. Butterworth, 1933) tells of the role of Evangelicals in this decisive activity. Charles H. E. Smyth has a worthwhile chapter on the Evangelicals in *The Church and the Nation* (New York: Morehouse-Barlow, 1963). Kathleen Heasman, *Evangelicals in Action* (London:

Geoffrey Bles, 1962) and John Stewart Reynolds, *The Evangelicals at Oxford, 1735-1871* (Oxford: Basil Blackwell, 1953) should also be of interest.

p. 78 Anglicanism, being established, naturally has been most studied, and we have an embarrassment of wealth. For general histories, one can recommend the comprehensive but cool work by the Bishop of Ripon, John R. H. Moorman, *A History of the Church in England* (London: A. and C. Black, 1953) or the lighter, fast-moving Stephen Neill, *Anglicanism* (Baltimore, Md.: Penguin Books, 1958). For its concentration on this period, Spencer C. Carpenter, *Church and People, 1789-1889* (New York: Macmillan, 1933) is still commendable, if slightly confusing.

Two somewhat specialized studies are Charles K. F. Brown, *A History of the English Clergy*, 1800-1900 (London: The Faith Press, 1953) and William L. Mathieson, *English Church Reform*, 1815-1840 (New York: Longmans, Green and Co., 1923). On the worship life of Anglicanism, two works stand out: Horton Davies, *Worship and Theology in England from Watts and Wesley to Maurice 1690-1850* (Princeton, N.J.: Princeton University Press, 1961) and its companion volume . . . *from Newman to Martineau, 1850-1900* (Princeton, N.J.: Princeton University Press, 1962). A High Church Lutheran from Sweden, Yngve T. Brilioth, shows much subtlety in his *The Anglican Revival* (New York: Longmans, Green and Co., 1933). This title brings us to the Oxford Movement.

There is only one way to begin a bibliographical note, and that is to say that the literature is overwhelming. That rubric fulfilled, I suggest as one means of getting at it, the readings in Eugene R. Fairweather, ed., *The Oxford Movement* (New York: Oxford University Press, 1964). Fairweather includes a good bibliography of the works by individual leaders and a basic book list beyond that. The most important additional study for our purposes is William George Peck, *The Social Implications of the Oxford Movement* (New York: Scribner's, 1933). Harold J. Laski also commented at some length on this subject in *Studies in the Problem of Sovereignty* (New Haven, Conn.: Yale University Press, 1917), pp. 69ff. It is hard to resist adding at least Geoffrey Faber's, *Oxford Apostles: A Character Study of the Oxford Movement* (London: Faber and Faber, 1933).

p. 80 I have made reference to 'the Cambridge Movement' as a code word for the revival of interest in æsthetics and building which focused on Gothic. James F. White, *The Cambridge Movement* (Cambridge: Cambridge University Press, 1962) is the first over-all study of the 'movement'. Sir Kenneth M. Clark's *The Gothic Revival* (London: Constable and Co., 1928) has a chapter on churches, and asks why Victorians chose Gothic. Basil F. L. Clarke, *Church Builders of the Nineteenth Century* (New York: Macmillan, 1938) sheds light on the topic; see also Peter Ferriday, ed., *Victorian Architecture* (Philadelphia, Pa.: J. B. Lippincott and Co., 1964), with its display of churches. The architecture of any age tells much about religious aspirations, and the Victorian times are no exception.

p. 80 Christian Socialism, like the Oxford Movement, was literary and well-defined – which is another way of saying that it has attracted an inordinate amount of attention. A major recent study is Torben Christensen, *Origin and History of Christian Socialism 1848-54 in Acta Theologica Danica, Vol. III* (Copenhagen: Universitats forloget i Aarhus, 1962). Christensen throws new light on Ludlow, particularly on continental and Roman Catholic influences. The well-received work by Charles E. Raven, *Christian Socialism, 1848-54* (London: Macmillan and Co., 1920), still merits reading. The theoretical background is covered in C. K. Gloyn, *The Church in the Social Order: A Study of Anglican Social Theory from Coleridge to Maurice* (Forest Grove, Oregon: Pacific University Press, 1942). Gilbert C. Binyon, *The Christian Socialist Movement in England: An Introduction to the Study of Its History* (New York: Macmillan, 1931) is a standard work.

For the consequences of Christian Socialism: Maurice B. Reckitt, *Maurice to Temple: A Century of the Social Movement in the Church of England* (London: Faber and Faber, 1947) and the excellent book by Peter d'Alroy Jones, *The Christian Socialist Revival, 1877-1914* (Princeton, N.J.: Princeton University Press, 1968).

p. 84 While my text concentrates on utilitarianism, that philosophy should be seen in the sequence of political theories; one way to study them is by reading Crane Brinton, *English Political Thought in the Nineteenth Century* (London: Ernest Benn, 1933). Like everything else from the late Professor Brinton's hand, this flows well and is easy to read. The bibliography was updated for a paperback edition in 1962, and it will serve to introduce individual theorists.

Two books with the same title introduce the main political and social theorists of the radical tradition; they are, not surprisingly, John W. Derry, *The Radical Tradition: Tom Paine to Lloyd George* (New York: St Martin's Press, 1967) and Richard H. Tawney, *The Radical Tradition* (New York: Pantheon Books, 1964). Some documents that relate to these pages are to be found in Alan L. C. Bullock and Maurice Shock, editors, *The Liberal Tradition from Fox to Keynes* (London: A. and C. Black, 1956).

For a study of attempts to relate the church to the political traditions, see Olive J. Brose, *Church and Parliament: the Reshaping of the Church of England, 1828-1860* (Stanford, California: Stanford University Press, 1959). It stresses the impact of politics on ecclesiastical life. For the opposite side of the story, the impact of church on politics, there is Donald O. Wagner, *The Church of England and Social Reform since 1854* (New York: Columbia University Press, 1930).

p. 86 The relation of Darwinism to the Churches has also attracted many scholars. For a warm-up, Milton Millhauser, *Just Before Darwin* (Middleton, Conn.: Wesleyan University Press, 1959) will serve. Charles Gillispie, *Genesis and Geology: A Study in the Relations of Scientific Thought, Natural Theology, and Social Opinion in Great Britain, 1790-1850* (Cambridge, Mass.: Harvard University Press, 1951) is about what its title suggests, and is a good followup to Millhauser. Loren C. Eiseley, a master of English prose, provides us with an elegant study of Darwinian consequences in *Darwin's Century: Evolution and the Men who Discovered it* (Garden City, N.Y.: Doubleday and Co., 1958).

p. 92 The comprehensive book on Victorian attitudes, based largely on the literature of the time, is Walter E. Houghton, *The Victorian Frame of Mind 1830-1870* (New Haven, Conn.: Yale University Press, 1957). Less crowded, more lively, and more controversial, is Gertrude Himmelfarb, *Victorian Minds* (New York: Alfred A. Knopf, 1968). The formal study of Victorian literature falls somewhat outside the range of my competence, and I have relied on these two works, among others; numerous quotations from authors of the period were purloined from their research for my 'Greek chorus' passages.

Three works on the novel will help guide interested readers into that limitless area: William H. Marshall, *The World of the Victorian Novel* (South Brunswick, N.J.: A. S. Barnes, 1967) (see especially the first chapter, 'The Empty Sanctuary and the English Novel'); U. C. Knoepflmacher, *Religious Humanism and the Victorian Novel: George Eliot, Walter Pater, and Samuel Butler* (Princeton, N.J.: Princeton University Press, 1965); and, directly to the point of this section, and incorporating a fine bibliography of novels, Margaret M. Maison, *The Victorian Vision: Studies in the Religious Novel* (New York: Sheed and Ward, 1962).

I have left for last a reference to the literature which parallels my own thesis, the subject of religious doubt and agnosticism. A standard but biased work is the two-volume, John Mackinnon Robertson, *A History of Free Thought in the Nineteenth Century* (London: Watts and Co., 1929). The Quaker Herbert G. Wood has crammed much information and good sense into a too-brief *Belief and Unbelief since 1850* (Cambridge: Cambridge University Press, 1955).

Basil Willey wrote two books of general interest on the nineteenth century, *Nineteenth-Century Studies: Coleridge to Matthew Arnold* (New York: Columbia University Press, 1949) and, more pertinently because it stresses doubters, *More Nineteenth Century Studies* (New York: Columbia University Press, 1956).

A. O. J. Cockshut has taken the doubters seriously, and the result is presented, in part, in his *The Unbelievers: English Agnostic Thought 1840-1890*. (New York: New York University Press, 1966). Beyond our chronological scope, but very much in the mood of this study, is Warren Sylvester Smith, *The London Heretics* 1870-1914 (London: Constable and Co., 1967). Be sure to consult the endpaper cartoon by secularist George Jacob Holyoake for a sarcastic view of the contending parties in 1883. Howard R. Murphy argues that the stirrings of doubt and discontent and liberation can be located already in the 1840s, in an article, 'The Ethical Revolt against Christian Orthodoxy in Early Victorian England' in *American Historical Review*, LV, No. 4, pp. 880-817 (July, 1955). Warren Sylvester Smith concludes with John Mac-Kinnon Robertson that by the decade of the seventies 'the turning of the balance of educated intelligence from current creed to unbelief' was discernible, so he picks up the story there.

Chapter IV

p. 95 Winthrop S. Hudson's *Religion in America* (New York: Scribner's, 1965) is a fair-minded general introduction to American religion in this and all periods. To Hudson, 'religion' means churches and synagogues, and he pays little attention to extra-ecclesiastical religious phenomena. William Warren Sweet's *The Story of Religion in America* (New York: Harper and Brothers, 1930) is regarded as a classic if slightly dull account, with accent on Protestantism and the frontier. Less classic, more dull, but equally detailed and often quite useful is Clifton E. Olmstead, *History of Religion in the United States* (Englewood Cliffs, N.J.: Prentice Hall, 1960). Jerald C. Brauer's *Protestantism in America* (Philadelphia, Pa.: Westminster Press, 1953) was designed for young people; it stresses the spirit of experiment in a biblical context.

Basic for any profound study of American religion are the two volumes, Nelson R. Burr, *A Critical Bibliography of Religion in America* (Princeton, N.J.: Princeton University Press, 1961) with their 1200 pages of bibliographical essays. Readers will also gain a sense of immediacy in pursuit of American religious history with H. Shelton Smith, Robert T. Handy, and Lefferts A. Loetscher (ed.), *American Christianity: An Historical Interpretation with Representative Documents* (New York: Scribner's, 1963); Volume II covers 1820-1960.

Three interpretive volumes, finally, will help the newcomer embark. A seminal volume was H. Richard Niebuhr, *The Kingdom of God in America* (Chicago: Willett, Clark and Co. 1937); Sidney E. Mead collected his essays written over the period of a decade in *The Lively Experiment* (New York: Harper and Row, 1963). One of the few attempts at describing something like secularization in America is William A. Clebsch, *From Sacred to Profane America* (New York: Harper and Row, 1968), on the transformation of the American dream. Readers will find points of contrast and of comparison in Clebsch's and my volumes.

p. 98 My thought at this point (the third path to the secular) is influenced by that of Ernest Gellner, *Thought and Change* (Chicago: University of Chicago Press, 1965). This often overlooked book relates industrialization to philosophy; pp. 123-125 introduce the picture of glacial moraine which shows up once or twice in the

172 The Modern Schism

present book. Gellner discusses the growth of civic religions.

p. 101 On statistics and religious growth in American history, see Edwin Scott Gaustad, *Historical Atlas of Religion in America* (New York: Harper and Row, 1962); see the bibliographical materials on nineteenth-century sources on page 165; there Daniel Dorchester, Robert Baird, Joseph Belcher, Israel Daniel Rupp, and other authors are cited.

p. 102 Among sociologists who study the effects of transformed symbols as a mode of American secularization are: Seymour Martin Lipset, *The First New Nation* (New York: Basic Books, 1963); J. Milton Yinger, *Sociology Looks at Religion* (New York: Macmillan, 1963); Robert Bellah, 'Civil Religion in America' in William G. McLoughlin and Robert N. Bellah (eds.), *Religion in America* (Boston: Houghton Mifflin, 1968); John L. Thomas, *Religion and the American People* (Westminster, Md.: Newman Press, 1963); Charles Y. Glock and Rodney Stark, *Religion and Society in Tension* (Chicago: Rand McNally, 1965); Thomas Luckmann, *The Invisible Religion* (New York: Macmillan, 1967); Gerhard Lenski, *The Religious Factor* (Garden City, N.Y.: Doubleday and Co., 1961). Most of them have contemporary interests, but they depict the legacy of the nineteenth-century shifts in America. Lipset is more historical as he speaks of 'all-pervasive' religiousness as a consistent trait of American religion accompanied by secularity, a persistent trait of the same. Yinger describes the process by which symbols are transformed and civil religions formed by laymen in spite of or with the help of the clergy. Luckmann has also influenced my thinking at this point. All these authors blunt the effect of ideological secular interpretations and stress America's peculiar 'mix'. While not written with America particularly in view, David Martin's 'Towards Eliminating the Concept of Secularization' in Julius Gould (ed.), *Penguin Survey of the Social Sciences* (Baltimore, Md.: Penguin Books, 1965), is helpful. The enduring historical study of the fusion of evangelical and constitutional realities is Ralph Henry Gabriel, *The Course of American Democratic Thought* (New York: Ronald Press, 1940).

p. 104 On the church and ministry at the end of the period (to see how institutions survived and thrived), Francis P. Weisenburger, *Triumph of Faith: Contributions of the Church to American Life, 1865-1900* (Richmond, Va.: William Byrd, 1962) and

Ordeal of Faith: The Crisis of Church-Going America, 1865-1900 (New York: Philosophical Library, 1959). Both books lack focus but they do gather information not easily accessible elsewhere.

p. 104 Robert T. Handy (ed.), *The Social Gospel in America* (New York: Oxford University Press, 1966) collects some of the writings of the leading Social Gospel thinkers; more on the social corrective to the individualism of the later evangelical period is available in James Dombrowski, *The Early Days of Christian Socialism in America* (New York: Columbia University Press); see also Charles Howard Hopkins, *The Rise of the Social Gospel in American Protestantism* (New Haven, Conn.: Yale University Press, 1940).

p. 105 On our 'sample family' the Beechers, see Barbara M. Cross, ed., *The Autobiography of Lyman Beecher* (Cambridge, Mass.: Harvard University Press, 1961); pp. 118ff. in Sidney Fine, *Laissez Faire and The General-Welfare State* (Ann Arbor, Michigan: University of Michigan Press, 1956); the chapter on 'Princes of the Pulpit' in Winthrop S. Hudson, *The Great Tradition of the American Churches* (New York: Harper and Brothers, 1953) provides other instances along with Beecher. Paxton Hibben, *Henry Ward Beecher: an American Portrait* (New York: George H. Doran, 1927) stresses Beecher's role as a reinterpreter of symbols at a time of change.

p. 105 Robert H. Bremner, *American Philanthropy* (Chicago: University of Chicago Press, 1960) provides an adequate bibliography along with a good general survey; some of the earlier merchant enterprisers and philanthropists are followed in Charles I. Foster, *An Errand of Mercy: The Evangelical United Front, 1790-1837* (Chapel Hill, N.C.: University of North Carolina Press, 1960); changes are evident by the time covered in *American Conservatism in the Age of Enterprise: A Study of William Graham Summer, Stephen J. Field, and Andrew Carnegie* by Robert Green McCloskey (Cambridge, Mass.: Harvard University Press, 1951).

p. 106 Howard Wayne Morgan (ed., *The Gilded Age: A Reappraisal* (Syracuse, N.Y.: Syracuse University Press, 1963) includes several chapters on these 'robber barons'. Louis M. Hacker, *The World of Andrew Carnegie, 1865-1901* (Philadelphia, Pa.: J. B. Lippincott and Co., 1968) is an excellent depiction of the age and its bibliography will be of help.

p. 109 By far the best book on the social and economic status and involvements of revivalists is William G. McLoughlin's *Modern Revivalism: Charles Grandison Finney to Billy Graham* (New York: Ronald Press, 1959); less comprehensive but also to the point is Bernard A. Weisberger, *They Gathered at the River: The Story of the Great Revivalists and Their Impact upon Religion in America* (Boston: Little, Brown and Co., 1958).

p. 109 Alan E. Heimert and Perry Miller (eds.), *The Great Awakening* (Indianapolis, Ind.: Bobbs-Merrill Co., 1967) collects documents of the First Great Awakening. Edwin Scott Gaustad, *The Great Awakening in New England* (New York: Harper and Brothers, 1957) is a convenient and succinct summary of this period, essential as background for nineteenth-century religious studies. Also noteworthy in this context are: Perry Miller, *Errand into the Wilderness* (Cambridge, Mass.: Harvard University Press, 1956) and Alan E. Heimert, *Religion and the American Mind: from the Great Awakening to the Revolution* (Cambridge, Mass.: Harvard University Press, 1966). The latter brings together great amounts of information but is marred somewhat by a thesis overstressing Calvinism and understressing Arminianism. A synthesizing history of the Second Great Awakening remains to be written, but one does well to begin on the eastern phase with Charles R. Keller, *The Second Great Awakening in Connecticut* (New Haven, Conn.: Yale University Press, 1942) and for the West, Whitney R. Cross, *The Burned-Over District* (Ithaca, N.Y.: Cornell University Press, 1950) and Catherine C. Cleveland, *The Great Revival in the West* Chicago: University of Chicago Press, 1916).

p. 110 Sidney E. Mead's essay, 'Denominationalism: The Shape of Protestantism in America', *op. cit.* is a widely accepted and well-reasoned summary of the formative changes of this period.

p. 112 Sidney E. Mead's *Nathaniel William Taylor, 1786-1858* (Chicago: University of Chicago Press, 1942) is one of the few major works to trace the subtle theological changes inside what was called Calvinism in this period.

p. 113 The literature on Church and state is, of course, enormous. Anson Phelps Stokes and Leo Pfeffer, *Church and State in the United States* (New York: Harper and Row, 1964) is a one-volume condensation of Stokes' earlier giant three-volume collection of information on the subject. A Protestant interpretation is to be found in Winthrop Hudson's *The Great Tradition of the American*

Churches. (New York: Harper and Brothers, 1953).

p. 115 On Evangelicalism's attitude to the intellect and to intellectuals, see Richard Hofstader, *Anti-Intellectualism in American Life* (New York: Alfred A. Knopf, 1963), a rather severe and judgmental study, and the unfinished work of the late Perry Miller, *The Life of the Mind in America* (New York: Harcourt, Brace and World, 1965).

p. 115 On science and the evangelicals, George H. Daniels, *American Science in the Age of Jackson* (New York: Columbia University Press, 1968) has much information, including biographies of early scientists, and is marked by informed comment on Evangelicalism and theology. My comment about a general absence of metaphysical philosophy at mid-century has to be qualified by the presence of Transcendentalism, which is dealt with later in the chapter. There were attempts to import German philosophy, particularly Hegelianism, as is evident in the narratives of Lloyd D. Easton, *Hegel's First American Followers* (Athens, Ohio: Ohio University Press, 1966) on the Ohio Hegelians and Paul R. Anderson, *Platonism in the Midwest* (Philadelphia, Pa.: Temple University Publications, 1963), on a club of Hegelians at Jacksonville, Illinois. St Louis also housed a Hegelian circle. Few of these had national influence in their time and were a bit later than the period under study here. In his chapter on philosophy in this period, Irving H. Bartlett finds little to talk about except Transcendentalism and Emerson in *The American Mind in the Mid-Nineteenth Century* (New York: Thomas Y. Crowell and Co., 1967).

If philosophers were few and far between, community dreamers and planners were not. Nor is the literature on them sparse. The place to begin a study of them is still Alice Felt Tyler; *Freedom's Ferment* (Minneapolis, Minn.: The University of Minnesota Press, 1944). See also Arthur E. Bestor, *Backwoods Utopias, The Sectarian and Owenite Phases of Communitarian Socialism in America*, 1663-1829) Philadelphia, Pa.: University of Pennsylvania Press, 1950) and Mark Holloway, *Heavens on Earth: Utopian Communities in America 1680-1880* (London: Turnstile Press, 1951). Recently two important nineteenth-century works were reprinted: John Humphrey Noyes, *History of American Socialisms* (first published in 1870; new edition from New York: Dover Publications, 1966) and Charles Nordhoff, *The Communistic Societies of the United*

States (first published in 1875; new publication, New York: Dover Publications, 1966). On the absence of profound atheists and the presence of small-town infidels, see Martin E. Marty, *The Infidel: Freethought and American Religion* (Cleveland, Ohio: Meridian Books, 1961).

p. 115 One student of denominational competition has been Walter Brownlow Posey; *Frontier Mission: A History of Religion West of the Southern Appalachians to 1861* (Lexington, Ky.: University of Kentucky Press, 1966) and *Religious Strife on the Southern Frontier* (Baton Rouge, La.; Louisiana State University Press, 1965) are both studies representative of his interest.

On millennial and prophetic primitivism, standard histories of the Seventh-Day Adventists (Millerites) and Latter-Day Saints (Mormons) are of most help. Le Roy E. Froom, *The Prophetic Faith of Our Fathers* is a four-volume world history from the Adventist point of view (Washington, D. C.: Review and Herald, 1946-54); a lively story of Mormon origins is Fawn M. Brodie, *No Man Knows My History: The Life of Joseph Smith, the Mormon Prophet.* (New York: Alfred A. Knopf, 1945).

p. 116 Arthur M. Schlesinger, Jr., *The Age of Jackson* (Boston: Little, Brown and Co., 1945) repeatedly focuses on the church's theocratic efforts in the time of Ezra Stiles Ely; see also the whole of chapter XXVII. John R. Bodo, *The Protestant Clergy and Public Issues,* 1812-1848 (Princeton, N.J.: Princeton University Press, 1954) is restricted by its neat categorical outline, but it does introduce the men and the issues. Of at least equal value is Charles C. Cole, Jr., *The Social Ideas of the Northern Evangelists, 1826-1860* (New York: Columbia University Press, 1954) from which I pirated a sequence of quotations about religion and economics later in this book. Bodo, Cole, and Charles I. Foster more than other authors describe the social, political, and economic setting of Evangelicalism.

p. 118 On immigration: of course, Oscar Handlin, *The Uprooted* (Boston: Little, Brown and Co., 1951); see also, Marcus Lee Hansen, *The Immigrant in American History* (Cambridge, Mass.: Harvard University Press, 1940) and the same author's *The Atlantic Migration,* 1607-1860 (Cambridge, Mass.: Harvard University Press, 1940); John Higham, *Strangers in the Land: Patterns of American Nativism,* 1860-1925 (New Brunswick, N.J.: Rutgers University Press, 1955) deals with a slightly later period. Ray A. Billington,

The Protestant Crusade, 1800-1860 (New York: Macmillan, 1938) remains the best study of nativist reaction.

Richard C. Wade, *The Urban Frontier: The Rise of Western Cities 1790-1830* (Cambridge, Mass.: Harvard University Press, 1959) is valuable for this study because it concentrates on pre-industrial urban areas; in several passages Professor Wade contrasts church growth in these cities with the more spectacular growth in villages and rural areas. For the slightly later period, when industrialism contributes to the growth of giant cities, see Blake McKelvey, *The Urbanization of America, 1860-1915* (New Brunswick, N.J.: Rutgers University Press, 1963), a book which is blessed with a fine bibliography, as Wade's is not. For some sources on the city towards mid-century, see Chapter Two in Charles N. Glaab. *The American City: A Documentary History* (Homewood, Ill.: Dorsey Press, 1963).

p. 118 Several books which will introduce the themes of enterprise, industry, and factory growth are: John Chamberlain, *The Enterprising Americans: A Business History of the United States* (New York: Harper and Row, 1963); Stuart W. Bruchey, *The Roots of American Economic Growth*, 1607-1861 (New York: Harper and Row, 1965); the older Thomas C. Cochran and William Miller, *The Age of Enterprise: A Social History of Industrial America* (New York: Harper and Row: revised edition, 1961) is still valuable. It was originally published in 1942. See also Joseph Dorfman, *The Economic Mind in American Civilization, 1606-1865* (New York: Viking Press, 1946).

p. 118 The story of early labour is told in Carl R. Fish, *The Rise of the Common Man, 1830-1850* (New York: Macmillan, 1937); Norman J. Ware, *The Industrial Worker, 1840-1860* (Boston: Houghton Mifflin, 1924); Joseph C. Rayback, *A History of American Labour* (New York: Macmillan, 1959). The story of radical organizers is told in Edward Pessen, *Most Uncommon Jacksonians: The Radical Leaders of the Early Labour Movement* (Albany, N.Y.: State University of New York Press, 1967).

p. 119 In addition to the above-mentioned books on labour, David Herreshoff's *American Disciples of Marx* (Detroit, Mich.: Wayne State University Press, 1967) reveals how impotent Marxist radicals were on the American scene; on Orestes Brownson, see Theodore Maynard, *Orestes Brownson: Yankee. Radical, Catholic*

(New York: Macmillan, 1943). Robert D. Cross, *The Emergence of Liberal Catholicism in America* (Cambridge, Mass.: Harvard University Press, 1958), in its earlier chapters, discusses Catholic participation in this phase of nineteenth-century culture. On Gibbons: John Tracy Ellis, *The Life of James Cardinal Gibbons, Archbishop of Baltimore, 1834-1921* (Milwaukee, Wisc.: Bruce Publishing Co., 1952) in two volumes goes into detail on Gibbons' relations to labour.

p. 122 The business attitudes of clergymen and laymen in the revivals of 1857-58 are carefully surveyed in Timothy L. Smith, *Revivalism and Social Reform in Mid-Nineteenth Century America* (New York: Abingdon Press, 1957), a book which regards revivalism favourably and stresses its role in shaping later social Christianity.

p. 122 See John G. Cawelti, *Apostles of the Self-Made Man* (Chicago: University of Chicago Press, 1965) and the source-book edited by Moses Rischin, *The American Gospel of Success* (Chicago: Quadrangle Books, 1965) for an introduction to the success cults. Earlier, Irvin G. Wyllie had surveyed the field in *The Self-Made Man in America* (New Brunswick, N.J.: Rutgers University Press, 1954).

p. 123 The stories of the deaths of Girard and Astor (with Vanderbilt, Morgan, Rockefeller, and Ford thrown in for good measure) are told in Sigmund Diamond, *The Reputation of the American Businessman* (Cambridge, Mass.: Harvard University Press, 1955).

p. 124 Andrew Carnegie, *The Gospel of Wealth*, has been published in the twentieth century under the editorship of Edward C. Kirkland (Cambridge, Mass.: Harvard University Press, 1962).

p. 125 The story of the flowering of New England and pre-Civil War literature has often been told; a few titles come to mind: Van Wyck Brooks, *The Flowering of New England* (New York: E. P. Dutton and Co., 1936); F. O. Matthiessen, *American Renaissance* (New York: Oxford University Press, 1941); Perry Miller, *Consciousness in Concord* (Boston: Houghton Mifflin, 1958); Perry Miller, (ed.) *The American Transcendentalists: Their Prose and Poetry* (Garden City, N.Y.: Doubleday and Co., 1957) will do for a start; it is not possible here to deal with the sizable literature on each of these figures.

p. 125 Carl Bode, *The American Lyceum: Town Meeting of the Mind* (New York: Oxford University Press, 1956) covers the subject of the lyceum; Eugene Exman has begun to write the history of Harper and Brothers, in *The Brothers Harper* (New York: Harper and Row, 1965) – which takes the story to 1853 – and in a general history for the 150th anniversary, *The House of Harper* (New York: Harper and Row, 1967). See also Warren S. Tryon, *Parnassus Corner: A Life of James T. Fields, Publisher to the Victorians* (Boston: Houghton Mifflin, 1963).

p. 126 On nature and technology, Leo Marx, *The Machine in the Garden* (New York: Oxford University Press, 1964) enlarges on Hawthorne's experience; see also Arthur A. Ekirch, Jr., *Man and Nature in America* (New York: Columbia University Press, 1963) also consult some chapters in Charles L. Sanford, *The Quest for Paradise: Europe and the American Moral Imagination* (Urbana, Ill.: University of Illinois Press, 1961); Roderick Nash, *Wilderness and the American Mind* (New Haven, Conn.: Yale University Press, 1967); Henry Nash Smith, *Virgin Land* (Cambridge, Mass.: Harvard University Press, 1950).

p. 127 Emerson, Hawthorne, Melville, and Poe are treated in portions of Morton G. and Lucia White, *The Intellectual Versus the City* (Cambridge, Mass.: Harvard University Press, 1962). For the story of the historians, see David W. Noble, *Historians Against History* (Minneapolis, Minn.: University of Minnesota Press, 1965).

p. 128 The themes of innocence and dismissal of the past have been treated frequently; I have profited most from R. W. B. Lewis, *The American Adam: Innocence, Tragedy, and Tradition in the Nineteenth Century* (Chicago: University of Chicago Press, 1955) and, for fiction only, David W. Noble, *The Eternal Adam and the New World Garden* (New York: George Braziller, 1968). Whereas Lewis concentrates on the mid-nineteenth century, Noble only begins there.

p. 128 Collections of writings by nineteenth-century visitors abound and accounts by individuals are often easily accessible in paperback; the literature is so vast that we cannot here list available writings of de Tocqueville, Martineau, and others. Among the collections are Oscar Handlin, (ed.), *This was America* (Cambridge, Mass.: Harvard University Press, 1949); George E. Probst, (ed.), *The Happy Republic* (New York: Harper and Row, 1962); Dan

Herr and Joel Wells (eds.), *Through Other Eyes* (Westminster, Md.: Newman Press, 1965) – on Catholicism – and Henry Steele Commager, (ed.), *America in Perspective* (New York: Random House, 1947).

p. 131 The two standard works on Protestantism in the developed industrial order are Aaron Ignatius Abell, *The Urban Impact on American Protestantism, 1865-1900* (Cambridge, Mass.: Harvard University Press, 1943) and Henry F. May, *Protestant Churches and Industrial America* (New York: Harper and Brothers, 1949). Abell's study of Catholicism is *American Catholicism and Social Action* (Notre Dame, Ind.: University of Notre Dame Press, 1960).

p. 133 This discussion of nationalism reflects the influence of Carlton J. H. Hayes, *Nationalism: A Religion* (New York: Macmillan, 1960), but for the American scene, see Hans Kohn, *American Nationalism* (New York: Macmillan, 1957). See also Yehoshua Arieli, *Individualism and Nationalism in American Ideology* (Cambridge, Mass.: Harvard University Press, 1964 (and Dorothy Dohen, *Nationalism and American Catholicism* (New York: Sheed and Ward, 1967).

p. 133 On the missionary sense in American expansionism, Frederick Merk, *Manifest Destiny and Mission in American History* (New York: Alfred A. Knopf, 1963). R. W. Van Alstyne, *The Rising American Empire* (New York: Oxford University Press, 1960) and Walter LaFeber, *The New Empire* (Ithaca, N.Y.: Cornell University Press, 1963) described some of the roots of the spirit of manifest destiny. A fine study of literature, religion, and mission is Ernest Lee Tuveson, *Redeemer Nation: The Idea of America's Millennial Role* (Chicago: University of Chicago Press, 1968).

p. 135 The most sane and serene of the many studies of Abraham Lincoln's religion (indeed, his theology) is William J. Wolf, *The Almost Chosen People* (Garden City, N.Y.: Doubleday and Co., 1959). See also the essay, 'The Union as Religious Mysticism' in Edmund Wilson, *Eight Essays* (Garden City, N.Y.: Doubleday and Co., 1954).

The less attractive subject of Protestant contributions to racist thinking is dealt with (for the earlier period) in Winthrop D. Jordan, *White Over Black* (Chapel Hill, N.C.: University of North Carolina Press, 1968). A more general history is Thomas F. Gossett, *Race: The History of an Idea in America* (Dallas, Texas: Southern

Methodist University Press, 1963). A case study is available in Andrew E. Murray, *Presbyterians and the Negro—A History* (Philadelphia, Pa.: Presbyterian Historical Society, 1966). William Sumner Jenkins, *Pro-Slavery Thought in the Old South* (Chapel Hill, N.C., University of North Carolina Press, 1935) is a durable study. Donald G. Matthews, *Slavery and Methodism* (Princeton, N.J.: Princeton University Press, 1965), also gets on to the subject of racial thinking.

p. 139 For a review of the religious situation in the American 'Enlightenment', several works are available: Herbert M. Morais, *Deism in Eighteenth Century America* (New York: Columbia University Press, 1934); G. Adolf Koch, *Republican Religion: The American Revolution and the Cult of Reason*: (New York: Henry Holt and Co., 1933) on positive religious adaptation, Conrad Wright, *The Beginnings of Unitarianism in America* (Boston: Beacon Press, 1955).

p. 140 C. Wright Mills has sketched an outline of steps for secularization of higher education in Part I, Chapter I, *Sociology and Pragmatism: The Higher Learning in America* (New York: Paine—Whitman Publishers, 1964). Other works which treat the subject include Laurence R. Veysey, *The Emergence of the American University* (Chicago: University of Chicago Press, 1965) and Frederick Rudolph, *The American College and University: A History* (New York: Alfred A. Knopf, 1962).

p. 141 Ruth Miller Elson, *Guardians of Tradition: American Schoolbooks of the Nineteenth Century* (Lincoln, Nebr.: University of Nebraska Press, 1964) is crowded with evidence concerning the part played by elementary texts in glossing over cultural change and transformation of values.

INDEX